The
Foster Care
Survival Guide

The Essential Guide for Today's Foster Parents

By Dr. John DeGarmo

THE FOSTER CARE SURVIVAL GUIDE: THE ESSENTIAL GUIDE FOR TODAY'S FOSTER PARENTS

1405 SW 6th Avenue • Ocala, Florida 34471 • Phone 800-814-1132 • Fax 352-622-1875
Website: www.atlantic-pub.com • Email: sales@atlantic-pub.com
SAN Number: 268-1250

Library of Congress Cataloging-in-Publication Data

Names: DeGarmo, John, 1969- author.
Title: The foster care survival guide : the essential guide for today's foster parents / by Dr. John DeGarmo.
Description: Ocala, Florida : Atlantic Publishing Group, Inc., [2018] | Includes bibliographical references and index.
Identifiers: LCCN 2017061620 (print) | LCCN 2018007798 (ebook) | ISBN 9781620235812 (ebook) | ISBN 9781620235805 (pbk. : alk. paper) | ISBN 1620235803 (alk. paper)
Subjects: LCSH: Foster home care—United States—Handbooks, manuals, etc. | Foster parents—United States.
Classification: LCC HQ759.7 (ebook) | LCC HQ759.7 .D437 2018 (print) | DDC 649/.145—dc23
LC record available at https://lccn.loc.gov/2017061620

Printed in the United States

PROJECT MANAGER: Danielle Lieneman
INTERIOR LAYOUT AND COVER DESIGN: Nicole Sturk

Reduce. Reuse.
RECYCLE.

A decade ago, Atlantic Publishing signed the Green Press Initiative. These guidelines promote environmentally friendly practices, such as using recycled stock and vegetable-based inks, avoiding waste, choosing energy-efficient resources, and promoting a no-pulping policy. We now use 100-percent recycled stock on all our books. The results: in one year, switching to post-consumer recycled stock saved 24 mature trees, 5,000 gallons of water, the equivalent of the total energy used for one home in a year, and the equivalent of the greenhouse gases from one car driven for a year.

Over the years, we have adopted a number of dogs from rescues and shelters. First there was Bear and after he passed, Ginger and Scout. Now, we have Kira, another rescue. They have brought immense joy and love not just into our lives, but into the lives of all who met them.

We want you to know a portion of the profits of this book will be donated in Bear, Ginger and Scout's memory to local animal shelters, parks, conservation organizations, and other individuals and nonprofit organizations in need of assistance.

– Douglas & Sherri Brown,
President & Vice-President of Atlantic Publishing

Table of Contents

Introduction

Foster parenting had become my life. I believed my husband and children felt the same way. After six years as a foster family, we had a photo made for our church directory with all of our family, including our foster children. We knew we could not allow this photo to be in the church directory due to the rules at that time so we had a second photo made of our family without the foster children for the directory.

I was so proud of the photo that included everyone in our family. The children were what my grandmother would have called "spit-shined." Their hair was combed perfectly, their faces were relaxed, their clothes were color-coordinated, and they all had adorable smiles. My husband was his handsome self. I looked at the photo on numerous occasions, but I never really looked at myself.

About a month after we got the photo, our Foster Home Development Worker came for her monthly visit. I couldn't wait to show her the photo. When I showed it to her, I did not get the positive response I was expecting. She asked me if I had looked at myself in the photo. I told her no, not really. She took my hand and told me to really look at myself. What I saw shocked me to my core. My hair was straggly and sticking up in odd places, I had huge very dark circles under my eyes, and no joy was showing on my face. That just could not be what I looked like! But it was.

Some serious soul searching and discussions with my husband and children followed that meeting with our family worker. She had talked to me about trying "to be all things to all children" and what that was doing not only to myself but also to my beloved family. I had a lot to learn about being a foster mom while ensuring my family was safe and happy, too. We owe our successful years as a foster family to that foster home worker.

At the time, our family was struggling to better understand how we were going to take care of ourselves so we could give our best to the children that joined our family through foster care and adoption. I could find few books that spoke to me in "foster parent language"about that very subject. Today, I am grateful to Dr. DeGarmo for writing such a book, a book written in "foster parent language." This book answers the questions we struggled with many times over our 27-year tenure as a family providing family foster care to 127 children and through the adoptions of four children into our family.

20 years of fostering led to many years of advocacy work on the local, state, and national levels. In my current role as the Executive Director of the National Foster Parent Association, I see this book serving as a component of the type of advocacy work we strive to do and struggle to accomplish each and every day for the foster parents, adoptive parents, and kinship caregivers serving the children and youth in the current foster care systems across the United States.

As you read through this book, you will find some quotes that speak to Dr. DeGarmo and they will speak to you too. Enjoying quotes that speak to foster parents is a shared joy for Dr. DeGarmo and myself. Here are a few I hope will speak to you as they have to me over the years:

> "I am not afraid to grieve. I am afraid of what would happen to these children if no one took the risk to love them."
>
> —Unknown

> "My children may not look like me, they may not have my nose, my eyes, or my smile, but the resemblance is there, you just may not see it. THEY HAVE MY HEART."
>
> —Kathy L.H. Mendoza

"Family means a love so deep there's no way to measure it ... and no need to."

—Unknown

"They don't care how much you know until they know how much you care."

—Unknown

"You never know when you are making a memory."

—Rickie Lee Jones

To close this book introduction, let me close with a quote that says it all for me. I hope and pray it says it all for you too.

"Every child deserves an irrational advocate!"

—Vera Fahlberg

Irene Clements , Executive Director of the
National Foster Parent Association

January 7, 2018

Preface

"How has your life changed while being a foster parent?"

This is a question I had been asked a great deal of late. Recently, I had been doing the rounds of radio and television interviews, all on the subject of being a foster parent. Like most people, many of the radio and television hosts had very little knowledge of what being a foster parent is really about. I would imagine many of your own friends and family members don't really understand what you do, either. Additionally, they likely do not understand how your life has changed.

I have said it many times, in many places: foster parenting is the hardest thing I have ever done. It is hard work. At the same time, it is also Heart Work. It is the most important job I have done, as well. I have been able to watch the lives of over 50 children change while living in my home.

My life has also changed in so many ways, in so many areas. Of the 50 plus children that have come to my home, come to live with my family, each has made me a better person and has made an impact on my life in some way.

I have learned to love deeper, more openly, and without abandon. I have learned to love each child that comes into my home in an unconditional manner and without reservation. I am no longer ashamed to tell people that I love them. I cry openly now and am no longer embarrassed when it happens. The saying that "real men don't cry" is rubbish to me. I have become an emotional cripple in that manner, yet in a healthy way, a way that I embrace.

Foster parenting has created a sense of urgency within me to make a difference in the lives of those in need. Perhaps it is because of the children's horror stories that I have been witness to and have watched come through my home. Regardless of the reason, I am able to see the pain and suffering in others and am better equipped to help them. To be sure, I have always had a desire to help others, but since I have become a foster parent to children who have suffered from abuse, neglect, and abandonment, all by those who profess to love them the most, their birth family members, I have felt compelled to help even more.

I have learned to forgive more. Love and forgiveness are two actions that are intertwined and cannot be separated. If we truly love others, then we need to forgive, as well. Without forgiveness, there is no love. When I was angry towards our foster teenager's mother, I was in no way sharing love. Instead, my stomach was in knots; I was one tense parent. I was shackled by my own inability to forgive someone, a prisoner to a debilitating emotion. Yet when I did forgive her, it felt like a weight was taken off my own shoulders. One of the amazing things about the act of forgiving others is that it allows us to better use our energies towards something that is more constructive, more positive. Forgiveness frees us from the forces of hate and evil, and instead allows us to draw closer to others and gives us more strength to do the work we are called to do. When we forgive the actions of our foster child's birth parents, not only are we showing love to them and empowering ourselves, we are also honoring our foster children.

As I write this, my wife and I have 10 children in our home. 10! We are not a group home, but sadly, in my area of the nation, there are far too few people willing to be foster parents, far too few who are willing to open up their homes and their families to children in need.

To be honest, there are times when my wife and I are tired, worn out, exhausted, and feel like we can't go on any further. There have been those times when we have been burned out and our family lives suffered. There have been those times when we have not cared for ourselves.

As a foster parent, you need to take care of yourself. You need to ensure that you are watching after yourself, finding the time you need for you, and the help you need to care for not only the children in your home, but for yourself and your family. If you do not, all that you do will suffer.

My friend, I am thankful for what you do each day. I am thankful that you are making sacrifices in your life in order to care for children in need, children in foster care. I am thankful that you have opened up your home and your family to children who need help, who need stability, and who need love. You are making a difference. Now, take care of yourself, as well!

—Dr. John DeGarmo

CHAPTER ONE

The Life of a Foster Parent

It was a difficult time for my wife and me, and we both felt drained physically and emotionally. Another child had left our family. Another child from foster care that had been living with us for several months was moving to another home. This time, it was a little different, and the pain of it lingered on for some time.

Little Devon came to our family late one night at 12:30 a.m., an emergency placement that was to be with us only for a day or so. A familiar claim for foster parents, that's for sure. The four-pound baby was on a heart monitor and a breathing machine, requiring around-the-clock monitoring. Fortunately for me, I was on a vacation and was able to look after the tiny infant at all times. He was so small that he could fit in one of my hands. To be sure, the first time I changed his diaper, I thought I might somehow break his small body. His weakened condition required that he be fed once an hour, every hour, 24 hours a day, as his tiny frame needed nourishment. His first few weeks with us left me in an almost zombie like state, exhausted from his hourly feeding and breathing treatments.

As expected, my wife and I quickly fell in love with little Devon, and when the child's caseworker informed us three months later that Devon would be available for adoption, my wife quickly jumped at the opportunity. I was a little hesitant, as this would be the seventh DeGarmo child, but as always, my heart quickly changed my thought process. Indeed, I began looking forward to the adoption of this little one into our family.

Sadly, Devon was not able to become a part of our family, and we were faced with our second failed adoption a month later. The child our family grew to love as one of our own moved to another foster home, one where his older sibling was, with foster parents who soon adopted both Devon and his older brother. I must share with you, the experience left me grief stricken. For days, there was a tremendous pain in my stomach, and I felt as if I would break into tears at any given moment. My wife was suffering, as well. Four days after Devon left our family, I walked into the bathroom after work, and found my wife crumpled on the floor, sobbing, heartbroken from the grief she felt.

So, why do we foster? Why do you and I take child after child into our families, only to have our hearts break time and time again when the child leaves our home? Why do we run ourselves to the point of exhaustion, looking after a house full of children on with insufficient sleep and energy? Quite simply, because there is a child out there, right now, that needs a home. There is a child out there, today, who needs a family and who needs to be loved. If you are like me, being a foster parent is the most rewarding thing you have ever done. Each child that has come through your home has made you a better person in some way: a better parent, a better spouse, and a better member of the community. You love being a foster parent, you love caring for the children in your home, and you love the opportunity to make a different in the life of a child in need.

It's OK to Say It's Hard

I often hear, on a weekly basis, that my wife and I are saints for caring for children in need and opening up our homes and hearts to kids in foster care. In no way, and in no fashion, am I a saint, and I believe that foster parents from all over would echo that sentiment. We are not saints. We become tired, worn down, and exhausted. We have our own frustrations and disappointments. There are times when we succeed, and there are times when we experience failures. We are not the perfect parents. We are simply trying our best to provide a home and family for a child who needs one and help a child in need.

Yet, the life of a foster parent is not always an easy one. In fact, it is OK to say that being a foster parent is hard.

It's OK to say that sometimes you just feel like no understands what you are going through.

Guess what. It's even OK to say that sometimes, you simply want to stop, that you can't do it any more, that you are just don't want to be hurt again.

Yes, foster parenting can be difficult. You see, I have been a foster parent for 15 years, now. Foster parenting, without a doubt, has been the hardest thing I have ever done. I cannot imagine a more difficult and challenging lifestyle. I have lived the life of a foster parent. I have had over 50 children come through my home. These children have been as young as 27 hours old and as old as 18 years of age. Some have stayed a day, while others have stayed up to two years. I have had up to 11 children in my home, and at one time had seven in diapers. To be sure, seven in diapers was one exhausting experience. I jokingly tell people that having seven in diapers at the same time should be illegal in all 50 states and every country.

Like so many foster parents, and very likely just like you, I often go to work so I can rest. Yes, work is more restful than it is in my house, as it is very likely in your own home. For you see, when we come home, we face the many needs of children facing anxieties and traumas, with the responsibilities of taking children to visitations with birth family members, to doctor appointments, to counseling and therapy sessions.

The outside world does not see the many challenges and struggles you may face on a daily, and sometimes hourly, basis. Your friends and family don't truly understand or appreciate what you are going through. Others see the children coming in and out of your home on a regular basis, and most find it a wonderful thing you are doing, but also may find it a little odd or strange and question why you do it.

You will often find yourself exhausted, both mentally and physically, and feel drained. There is very little money available to help you, and you may not be reimbursed for all the money you spend on your foster child. The job will require you to work 24 hours a day, seven days a week, with no time off. You will probably feel overworked and underappreciated. You will work with children who are most likely coming from difficult and harmful environments. Some of these children will have health issues, some will come with behavioral issues, and some will struggle with learning disabilities. Many times, the children you work with will try your patience, and leave you with headaches, frustrations, disappointments, and even heartbreaks. There is a reason why many people are not foster parents, as it is often too difficult. There have been those times where my heart has broken when a child left my home. There have been those moments when I have questioned whether or not I was making a difference. There have been those times when I have grown frustrated with the system, as I have had to stand by and watch some of the children in my home go back to environments and situations which I knew that were not healthy or safe. To be sure, I have also watched my wife's own doubts and her desire to no longer foster, as her heart had been broken numerous times, as well, from the many children she had grown to love, only to see them return to homes where the children were once again placed in jeopardy.

It is the same for so many foster parents who have shared their stories with me. I have heard from foster parents who lose sleep each night for weeks and months on end, trying to calm and soothe a baby who was born addicted to crack, heroin, or meth. I have heard from foster parents who have been yelled at on a daily basis from foster teenagers who are so emotionally upset by their own experiences that they take it out on their foster parents. I have heard from those who have been told one day they could adopt their foster babies, only to be told another day that the baby would return instead to a biological family member the child had never met. The stories are countless, the stories are heartbreaking, and the stories are never ending. Surely, there is no earthly reason to be a foster parent. So, why do we do it? For many, like my wife Kelly, we are answering a call.

Yes, my friend. I give you permission. It is truly okay to say that it is hard. It is OK to say that you can't do it anymore. It is OK to step away for a while and take a break: say no to a placement and allow yourself time to recover and fill that cup back up again.

Yet, if you are like me, you continue to care for children because the need is so strong. After all, right now, as you read this, there is a child in need of someone to say, "I care. I will take care of you. I will help you. I will love you."

When we care for children in foster care and bring them into our homes and families, we help change their lives. Yet, at the same time, our lives are changed, as well, and they are changed for the better. I have become a much better person for each child that has come through my home.

Do I sometimes want to say I can't do this anymore? Yes, sometimes I do. Guess what? That's normal. It is normal to question at times if you are truly making a difference. It is normal to feel frustrated by the situations you experience. It is normal for you to feel so very tired. It is normal to feel like you want to quit at times.

The Joys of Being a Foster Parent

The rewards and joys of being a foster parent are endless. I have been able to watch a four-year-old girl smile for the first time. I mean, truly smile, for the first time in her life, after years of horrific sexual abuse by her grandfather. Then there was the blessing of helping a six-year-old boy learn how to laugh, slowly at first, as if he were too nervous to allow himself to find joy in life; a six-year old boy who had only known harsh, physical abuse by both his parents, those sworn to protect and love him. There was the joy of helping a 17-year-old boy, abandoned by his mother, discover that he does have value and worth in his life, that he is important, and that he can accomplish great things. After living with us for nine months, we had the joy of watching this 17-year-old boy graduate from high school and enroll in college, thus beating the odds against him.

Foster parenting has been a tremendous gift to me. And I bet it has for you, as well.

Perhaps you have the desire to help out children who suffer from abuse or neglect; maybe you feel compassion for children who face malnutrition or drug-related problems passed on from a mother's addiction. Possibly, your heart goes out to those children who are rejected by those who were supposed to love them most. After all, you feel that every child deserves the right to be in a healthy and supportive home, and most importantly, every child deserves to be loved unconditionally. As a foster parent, you have the opportunity to help these children in need. When you foster a child, not only do you invest in the future and well-being of a child, you are also changing the life of that child.

To be sure, there have been those placements that have been more difficult and more challenging than others, placements that have left both my wife and I weary and exhausted. Sometimes, we may not be able to save a child from horrible and tragic experiences before they come to live with us. Yet, we are given the chance, as foster parents, to save them from experiencing other future horrors and taking them away from dangerous situations. Without a doubt, this is a joy itself. As a foster parent, indeed, as a parent, you are making a difference! You are saving a child from harm! It is my hope that you continue caring for children in foster care. There are so many children in care, yet so few willing to help.

My own heart is full. Through the tears of grief and sorrow and the joys and laughter, I have found that my own heart is rather like the Grinch's. Remember in the classic 1966 Christmas cartoon "How the Grinch Stole Christmas," when his heart grew so large it burst out of the x-ray device? That is how my own heart is. I have experienced so many diverse and intense emotions through the years that my heart is flowing over with love for all.

JULIANNA'S STORY

Building my family through foster care is a unique experience. You receive a call and within hours, you are the parent of one or more children. These children are strangers and you begin your journey of getting to know them. Over time you learn their fears, quirks and who they are. You begin falling in love with these little strangers, not knowing if you have months, years, or forever with them.

I look at my current tribe and wonder what will next year bring? We know that Baby Boy will be forever ours, as we await a final date and the details of adoption? I am often asked about the other three, if they will ever be forever ours. The hard reality of fostering is that we don't get to choose. More often than not, I have come across families whose hearts are broken when they don't get to keep those Littles they desperately love.

Being a foster parent is risky and painful. There is very little security in this world when it comes to love. Being a foster parent means you don't get the nine months of pregnancy to prepare, there is no maternity leave, and you don't get to soak in those first moments post-birth. We often miss the first moments or years of our children's lives. We get all of the hurt, fears, and aches; we grieve with them, fight for them, and let them go, even when we don't want to. We say goodbye more often than we want. We perfect the hello to strangers, opening our home to those hurting Littles.

This love is risky, this love has broken me, and this love has changed me. My tribe of seven is my daily reminder that the risk is worth it. The price tag is high but loving them well means my heart never finds that place of complete peace, no parent ever finds that place.

Being a foster parent is hard, the hardest thing I have ever done, in fact. Being a foster parent is messy. Being a foster parent is chaotic. It is also the most life-giving, joy-inducing, soul-satisfying thing I have ever done. It is in the brokenness of it all I have found contentment, I have found joy, I have found grace and compassion, and I have found more love when I thought there was none left to give.

—Julianna

We Can't Save Them All

I understand that we can't save all the foster children out there who need help. Friends and family have told me this, as they question why I continue to bring children into my home and into my family.

Yet, it is like the familiar Starfish story.

A father and son were walking along a beach at sunrise after a huge storm. When they stepped onto the beach, they were met with thousands of starfish littering the beach, hundreds in each direction. The boy bent down and picked up a starfish, throwing it far into the ocean. Again and again, he repeated the action. After watching his son for some time, the father asked, "Son, what are you doing?"

"I'm throwing these starfish back into the ocean," the young boy answered.

"I see. But why are you doing this?" the father asked.

"When the sun comes out and starts warming up the beach, the starfish will all die. I have to throw them back into the water."

"But son, you can't save all of these starfish. You can't possibly make a difference."

The boy stopped for a moment to take in his father's words, then bent down, and picked up another starfish in his hand, before throwing it as far as he could back into the ocean. Turning to his father with a large grin spreading across his face, he simply said, "It made a huge difference for that one!"

And it can make a huge difference for each child from foster care we bring into our home.

Being a foster parent is often the hardest thing we do. After all, each time a new foster child comes into our family, there are new challenges, as each placement, each child, is unique. Every placement will be different, and it will not become routine; some placements may even be unsettling. We do not have a "normal" lifestyle, to be sure, and we make many sacrifices as we bring children in need and in trauma into our family.

Yet, we are changing lives, while our own lives are being changed. There is a good chance that in the future, the foster child we cared for may not remember our names. There is a good chance that in the future, the foster child we care for may not remember our faces. But for so many children in foster care, each foster child who comes through our homes will remember one thing; that for a period in his life, he was loved, and some day down the road, he will blossom into something better because of it.

And we will be better because of the child, as well.

CHAPTER TWO

Burnout and Stress:
Living an Exhausting Lifestyle

Without a doubt, foster parenting is a very rich and rewarding, yet challenging, lifestyle. There should be no doubt that it is a lifestyle. You live a very different style of life than most of your friends and family do. As foster parents, we are able to truly make a difference in the lives of children. We are able to help bring a smile to a child who has never known a moment of happiness. We are able to protect children from harm, provide opportunities and environments where they can find hope, help them heal, and of course, share love with them. For us, for you and me as foster parents, our own lives are equally changed, as well. If you are like me, being a foster parent is something I not only love to do, but also feel called to do.

Yet, at the same time, it is the most difficult job, if you will, that I have ever done. If you put aside the fact that we, as foster parents, are caring for children who have suffered great trauma and anxiety in our home, there are the responsibilities of visitations, court appearances, doctor appointments, challenges with schools, behavior issues, working with birth parents and biological family members, meetings with case workers, paperwork, and the day-to-day challenges that come with caring for a child in your home who is suffering in some way. There are times when you and I, my friend, just feel tired, exhausted, worn down, and burned out.

To be sure, burnout is a very real condition that foster parents experience. The Merriam-Webster Dictionary defines burn out as:

> "Exhaustion of physical or emotional strength or motivation usually as a result of prolonged stress or frustration"

Dictionary.com gives us this definition:

> "Fatigue, frustration, or apathy resulting from prolonged stress, overwork, or intense activity."

Have you ever felt that way? Chances are, there have been times in your life when you have. We all have those times in our lives when we feel that we need a little boost, a little extra. We feel tired and perhaps even disillusioned or depressed. There are those times when we feel that we just can't go on anymore with the daily routine and feel as if everyone else's needs and wants are being met, that the demands of everyone else are overshadowing our own. These feelings and these emotions are normal and happen to each of us. There is no age, no profession, and no income level that escapes burnout.

Yet, when you do all that you do as a foster parent; when you care for children in need 24 hours a day in your home, seven days a week, 365 days a year, the possibility of becoming burned out can increase. Let's be honest now. Foster parenting can be time consuming, and it is exhausting. It can be physically, mentally, and emotionally draining. If you are like me, I am sure that you put all of yourself into the children living in your home, as your family. You are emotionally invested in these children, and you love them with all that you have. My friend, as you care for these children, as you meet their needs, as you love them with all that you have, many times your own needs are not being met. There are many times as a foster parent myself that I feel powerless, that I feel helpless, and feel that I just don't have the support that I need.

Several years ago, I was there. I was burned out. My wife and I had a sibling group of five children in our home; five children who had suffered immensely, and whose needs were incredibly high. One suffered from Reactive Attachment Disorder, a disorder that prevents a person from forming healthy relationships with others, another had been sexually abused at an early age, while another was filled with immense anger. All five struggled in school, both academically and behavior-wise. The children also suffered from poor nutrition when they came to us and had poor health. On top of that, their birth mother was in the stage of denial, refusing to acknowledge her own choices in life and what those circumstances were. She placed the blame solely upon the foster care system and upon my wife and me. Oh, did I mention that we also had our own six children, as well? Yes, 11 children in the house. My wife and I were overwhelmed with all that we had to do. Between the cooking and cleaning, between the doctor's appointments and soccer practices, between the visitations and homework, we both had our own full-time jobs. Yes, as you can imagine, we both struggled to find time for each other, let alone ourselves.

I remember it vividly. It was early one morning, and I had crawled out of bed, weary from yet another night of little sleep. I was walking up the stairs to wake some of the children for school, and I found that I just didn't have the energy to sing my good morning song that I greet each child with daily. I stopped in the middle of the stairs and sat down. A heavy sigh escaped me, rolling through my entire body.

"I'm just so tired," I said aloud. "I can't do this anymore."

It was as if there all the energy in my body had been sucked out of me, and I felt that I had hit a brick wall. There was pressure on my shoulders, my stomach felt knotted, and my heart just hurt. I was burned out.

Burnout is not something that happens all at once. One does not simply wake up one morning, burned out. Indeed, it is a condition that happens slowly, over time, which can make it even more difficult to recognize. To be sure, many people do not recognize that they are becoming burned out until they hit that wall, so to speak.

So, what does burnout look like? Let's briefly look at the signs of burnout:

- Forgetfulness
- Lack of sleep/insomnia
- Fatigue
- Anxiety
- Lack of appetite
- Chest pains
- Shortness of breath
- Dizziness
- Headaches
- Fainting
- Depression
- Anger
- Isolation
- Apathy
- Lack of productivity

It is apparent from this list that being a foster parent is both an exhausting and emotional job, one that demands much of our attention, our time, and our emotions. Burnout is very real for foster parents. Let's look at what Julianne has to say about her own experience with burnout.

JULIANNE'S STORY

My husband and I had been foster parents for five years. During that time, we had 13 kids come through our home. We loved each of them, and gave all that we had to them. We both loved being foster parents and felt that it was a calling.

The first few years, we managed. It was hard, but we managed. We didn't have any help, as it was just the two of us, taking care of lots of kids who had special needs in our home. One little boy that stayed with us for almost two years was so full of anger. He had been severely beaten by his stepfather for much of his young, little life and then was placed with us when he was 7 years old. For the next two years, he would throw tantrums, break things in the house, and scream and yell at us. We knew that our love was not going to be enough to help him, so we took him to a professional therapist twice a week. After a while, we did begin to see some signs that it was helping, but still, the rages and fits of anger continued.

For my husband and me, it seemed as if we had to walk on eggshells around him. We never knew what would set him off on one of his screaming bouts. When he became angry and started screaming, sometimes it would take up to two hours for him to settle down. We are worn out, and we are tired. There are days when I just feel like I can't continue being a foster parent to this little boy. We love him. It's just that he is wearing us out, and there is very little joy in our house, right now. I just don't have any energy anymore, and my husband seems to have fallen into some kind of depression. Is this what it's like to be burned out? We need to make some changes, soon, for the mental health everyone in our home.

—Julianne

One of the keys to preventing burnout is awareness. Julianne recognized that she and her husband were experiencing burnout. Once you are aware that you are truly exhausted and facing burnout, you can then take steps to better care for yourself. If you are feeling exhausted, run down, depressed, unmotivated, hopeless or powerless, or even feel like running away, you may be experiencing burnout. Changes need to be made, just as Julianne suggested, otherwise you will not only suffer, but your marriage, your family, your children, and even your job will suffer, as well.

Compassion Fatigue

A very real condition for foster parents and caregivers is Compassion Fatigue, also known as Secondary Traumatic Stress, or STS. Dr. Charles Figley states that Secondary Traumatic Stress is "the natural consequent behaviors resulting from knowledge about a traumatizing event experience by a significant other. It is the stress resulting from helping or wanting to help a traumatized or suffering person." As foster parents, we are likely to experience some sort of emotional or physical response to the variety of stresses and anxieties when we care for those who have suffered from abuse, neglect, and trauma. Indeed, we are often at risk of STS, or Compassion Fatigue, as we not only work with children who have suffered trauma and anxiety, but live with these children 24 hours a day. It should come as no surprise to what one study found. According to a recent study by the

University of Bristol's Hadley Centre for Adoption and Foster Care, Compassion Fatigue is a condition that is widespread among today's foster parents.

There are several reasons why we, as foster parents, are at particular risk for Compassion Fatigue. Let's take a look at them.

Empathy

If you are like me, you feel for these children. You feel their pain, you feel their suffering. You take it on board, upon your shoulders and into your heart. My wife has told me countless times over the course of several years that she was not going to be a foster parent anymore due to the high level of grief and loss she feels when the children she has come to love leave our home. However, when the phone call comes, and she hears the story of a particular child who needs a home, she always says yes to the placement. She feels empathy for these children, just as you do. Yet as we feel for these children and their pain, we may over-empathize or over-identify with the children, and place ourselves at risk of internalizing their pain and trauma. I often do this myself.

Personal Trauma

I once spoke to Julie, a foster parent, who had suffered great trauma and abuse herself as a child. As tears rolled freely down her face, Julie told me that she had been raped several times by her older cousin when she was between the ages of seven and nine. She came from a family that did not discuss such things, and when she tried to approach members of the family, it was swept under the carpet. She never was able to find the therapy or help she needed. Years later, when Julie was a foster parent, a young girl was placed into her home, a young girl who had been raped by a member of her family. As this foster mother cared for the little one in her home, Julie's own trauma from her personal history resurfaced, triggering feelings and pain she had tried to forget and never really addressed.

Perhaps you are like Julie in some way. Perhaps you have experienced a traumatic event in your life or have suffered from personal loss. When you care for others who have experienced trauma similar to your own, your own past experience might be triggered, making you more at risk for internalizing the trauma of the child you are looking after.

Lack of Recovery Time

There is no mistaking the fact that there are not enough foster parents, certainly not enough to care for the increasing number of children being placed into foster care. That's why foster parents, just like you, are taking in more and more children into our homes. When one child leaves our home and family, for whatever reason that might be, we often quickly get a phone call, asking if we can take another placement and another child, leaving us little time to breathe, to recover, and to grieve, if need be.

When we do this, we do not allow ourselves the time to recover. We do not allow ourselves the opportunity to distance ourselves so we can heal, and we are not allowed "time off" from an emotionally, mentally, and physically demanding lifestyle. Instead, we continue to care for children who are in such need of all that we have. We continue to listen to the horror stories these children have lived through, and we continue to hear, over and over again, similar stories form the children who come in and out of our homes. This not only wears you down and perhaps burns you out, but is also increase the risk for you of STS.

Take Time for Yourself

As a foster parent, you **need** to take care of yourself. You **need** to ensure that you are watching out for yourself, finding the time you need for you, and the help you need to care for not only the children in your home, but for yourself and your family. If you do not, all that you do will suffer.

I know of some people who become so engrossed in being a parent and taking care of children that their own personal identity disappears over time. Now, being a parent is a wonderful calling and a gift from above. Yet you as a person, as an individual, are just as much a gift. Don't neglect who you are and what makes you special. After all, your spouse fell in love with you for who you are! Try to engage in your hobbies and interests as often as you can. Go out to lunch with friends. Read some books for enjoyment or for self-help. Don't forget some personal quiet time, as well. For me, I often find this as I drive to and from work. I am amazed at how lovely silence sounds when I turn off the radio and allow my thoughts to wander. I also use this time for prayers, as well. If you keep yourself happy and in a good mood, it will help ensure that you are in a better mood and spirits for your foster child, your spouse, and your family.

Sometimes, taking time for yourself also means saying "no" to the next phone call, the next placement. It is OK to say "no" once in a while as a foster parent. It is OK for you to take time for yourself, your spouse, and your family. It is OK to re-charge those batteries. It's OK to take some time off to grieve the loss of a child from foster care in your home, and in your life. It's OK to take some personal time, each day, for mediation, prayer, or spiritual time for yourself. One of the ways to treat burnout is simply to rest from time to time. Indeed, foster parents **do** need rest and a time of reprieve, every now and then.

Remember to "Be in the Moment"

Far too often, I spend too much time looking ahead to what I have to do. With all of the responsibilities as a foster parent, father, husband, as well as my work commitments and responsibilities, I find that I spend far too much time planning and worrying about all that needs to be done. There are times when I feel overwhelmed. There are also those times when I allow myself to worry what might happen to a child that has left my home and family. I worry for their safety, their future, their well-being. There are even those moments when I feel anger towards a decision made by the court system regarding a child that I am caring for, a decision that I might not agree is in the best interest of the child. I imagine that you have the same experiences from time to time. You worry too much about the future. You grow concerned about what has not happened yet. You allow yourself to become overwhelmed with these feelings and these anxieties. My friend, that's normal, and it is easy to do.

Instead, we need to remember to stay in the moment, to focus on the here and now, instead of what might happen or what could be. When we worry about what might happen in the future, we lose the chance and the opportunity to embrace and enjoy what is happening in the present. When we allow our worries and concerns to overwhelm us about future events, we do not allow ourselves to be helpful to those around us in the present moment. As foster parents, we can't care for, help, teach, and love the children living with our family, children that need us to be with them right now, in the moment, if we are overwhelmed with things we have no control over tomorrow, next week, or next year.

Let your heart break

You have probably heard the same thing I have heard, over and over again. They tell me, "Dr. John, I couldn't do what you do. It would hurt too much to give the kids back." I reassure them that is how it is supposed to be. Our hearts are supposed to break for these children — that means we are giving them what they need the most: someone to love them with all their heart.

Now, there are those who say that you, as a foster parent, should not get too attached. There are those who might suggest to you that they are really not your children. There are even those who might advise you that you need not become too emotionally invested in the children because they are bound to go back home. The truth, as you most likely know, is the opposite. We do love them as our own, and we experience feelings of grief and loss when a child leaves, as we shall examine in much more detail in Chapter 4. Yet, it is healthy for us to become emotionally invested and attached to the children in our home. If we do not become attached, and hold ourselves at arm's distance, so to speak, and try to protect ourselves, we will not be able to help the ones we are trying to care for.

Exercise, Diet, and Sleep time

Sure, you feel worn out, exhausted, and have a lack of energy. You feel as if you simply do not have any energy whatsoever. Yet, exercise goes a long ways towards treating burnout. Studies indicate that exercise is able to act as a sort of antidepressant medication, in that it helps treat moderate depression. Furthermore, when you exercise regularly, it also helps to prevent future burnout. You see, when we exercise, it helps to do all kinds of wonderful things to our brain. There is neural growth, endorphins are released, strong chemicals run through our brain that help us to feel great and revitalize our well emotional well-being. Along with that, it simply serves as a distraction to what is troubling us. Instead of focusing on all of our worries and concerns, we are instead focused on walking up that next hill, running that extra mile, lifting even more weights, or whatever type of exercise and workout you chose to begin with. Plus, as my wife tells me, it allows us to have a break from the norm and gives us some quiet time.

Speaking of my wife, she is a doctor of nutrition. In our home, it is all organic, all-natural foods. None of that processed stuff on our shelves. If you have heard me speak at a conference or event, you know of my love for chocolate chip cookies, frozen pizzas, and sugary cereals. Yet, I can also tell you that I feel so much better when I cut out that junk food and eat healthy. According to the other doctor in my house, my wife reassures me that when I eat the foods I enjoy eating, it leads to lack of energy and a crash in my mood. So, I have learned to reduce my sugar intake, eat a great and healthy breakfast, and drink up to eight glasses of water a day, plus follow a regular, healthy diet. Make no mistake, this has helped me immensely, and is a strong contributor to treating burnout.

As a foster parent, you are probably asked when you sleep. We both know that finding sleep when you care for children, both your own and foster children, can be a challenge at times. When we are burned out, we may have trouble sleeping, or we may even sleep too much, as we feel like we just can't get out of bed or make it through the day. Getting a good night's sleep is essential to our health, our well-being, our productivity, and of course, to treat burnout.

Patience is a Virtue

MICHAEL'S STORY

Our 13-year-old girl has really tested my patience. She has been in our home for nine months, and each day has been a struggle. I understand that she came from a family where she was both abused and neglected, and I certainly feel for her and have compassion for her. But, she really tests us, every day. She is in trouble at school just about every day. She lies to my wife and me. She steals things from my wife's purse, and once even from a store. Every time we try to sit down and have a talk with her about her behavior, she screams at the two of us, runs into her room, and slams the door. Sometimes, she will just scream at us for long periods of time. If you were to say that I have just about lost patience with her, you would be about right.

—Michael

I imagine that there are a lot of foster parents who have walked in the same shoes that Michael and his wife have. I know that I have before, a time or two. There have been times when I have had to control my emotions, control my anger and frustration towards the child and the situation.

When we lose our control or lose our patience with a child, we lose control over the situation itself. When children see us lose control, it may suggest to them that the response they chose was the right one. It is important to remember that many children in foster care have never been in an environment where issues are addressed in a calm and rational manner, but instead in one of anger and hostility. Your own loss of patience and control reinforces to them that this response is normal, and acceptable. When a child in your home is trying your patience, as the saying goes, try and remain calm. Respond to the child in a calm fashion, with compassion and patience. Not only will you show the child that you can maintain control, you will also teach the child appropriate ways to hold discussions. Furthermore, it will help your own anxiety and stress level, helping you prevent future burnout.

If you are struggling with maintaining your own patience, go ahead and call your own time out. Don't be afraid or let your ego object to asking your spouse or partner to step in and take over a situation if you are becoming too frustrated or feel that you are you are losing control of your own emotions. Tell the child that you will talk about it at a later time, allowing both you and the child to cool off. Step outside or into another room and give yourself time to count to 10. Any of these are positive ways to de-escalate a situation.

Don't Take it Personally

There have been those times when some of the children living with my family have been disrespectful to me, have called me every name in the book, and have been downright mean-spirited towards my wife and me. Does my blood pressure rise, as a result? Yes, sometimes it does, and at times, it is difficult on all of us. To be sure, when a child calls you names, pushes your buttons, disobeys you, and treats you poorly, it is difficult not to take it personally. You may become angry; that's normal.

Yet, as a foster parent, it is important for all of us to remember that the child is most likely not attacking you personally. Children in foster care are often afraid, hurting, and in emotional pain. For so many children, they simply do not know how to process the many feelings and emotions that engulf and enwrap them. They are unsure how to appropriately release these pent up feelings, emotions, and anxieties and simply lash out instead. Lash out at you. Lash out at me. My friend, that's okay. You and I are simply the recipient of the pain and trauma that they suffer from. It is important for us not to take it as a personal attack. So, how do we do that? How do we prevent this from leading to burnout?

First, we need to remember that it isn't really about us. The child has been abused, neglected, abandoned. There is a reason why the child living in your home has been placed into foster care. He is hurting. It's not about us. It's about the child and his pain. Even when he is yelling, "I hate you!" and slamming the door, it's about the child. His anger and emotion may be directed at you, but it's not truly about you. Instead, his anger and pain come from someplace else.

When your buttons are being pushed, it is important to remember that you are the mature one; you are the adult and the parental figure. Resist yelling back; don't give in to the temptation to respond in anger. Try to not respond emotionally. Instead, focus on the child's behavior and not his emotion. Respond to why he is feeling this way, not to the words he may be yelling at you.

Your Own Support Group

I have said it over and over again; no one truly understands a foster parent like another foster parent. That's why it is important to surround yourself with a support group of fellow foster parents, especially when you are feeling burned out. There are a number of foster parent support groups and associations across the nation. A few of these organizations may be national ones, while many others are comprised of foster parents just like you. Either way, you will benefit from aa support organization, as they will provide you with not only support, but information, fellowship, and important insight that will help you be a better foster parent.

I know of some people that become so engrossed in being a parent and taking care of children that their own personal identity disappears over time. Don't neglect who you are and what makes you special. After all, your spouse fell in love with you for who you are! When foster parenting becomes too stressful, everyone around you — you, your family, and your foster child — will a feel the effects. Thus, one of the most important reminders for you, as a foster parent, is to take care of yourself, physically, mentally, and emotionally. If you neglect yourself, your family will suffer as a result. Finding time for you will not be easy, but it is very essential. Make time to do something you enjoy and that you find relaxing. Spend time with some friends, perhaps over lunch or dinner. Do not neglect your own personal health; make sure you get plenty of exercise regularly and eat healthy. If you take time for yourself, you will help to ensure your well-being as you care for others in your own home.

CHAPTER THREE

Meltdowns, Anxiety Attacks, and Disobedience

"We don't talk like that, Jimmy," I said. Sitting across the kitchen table from my nine-year-old foster son, a warm smile spread across my face. I was trying to be as compassionate and as understanding as I could with the troubled young child. Jimmy just looked down at the table, refusing to meet my eyes. I could see the different emotions etched across his face, as his eyes reflected a mixture of anger and question, and his forehead was wrinkled in confusion. Only 10 minutes ago, our foster child had called my son a bad name, one filled with profanity and ugliness. My wife was in the other room, trying to console my son, who was confused himself. Just earlier, the two had been playing together like old friends. Without warning, Jimmy grew suddenly angry, as rage filled his tiny frame. In a bout of anger, he lashed out at our son, cursing him and throwing the basketball at him.

"Well, my parents always did," he said with defiance.

"I understand, Jimmy, but we don't in our home. Those words are just not very nice." I replied. "Have you ever heard the phrase, 'Sticks and stones may break my bones, but names will never hurt me'?"

"Yeah," he said, his eyes still looking down at the table.

"Well, I bet you know that those words aren't true, aren't they Jimmy? Words do hurt. They hurt a lot more than sticks and stones." At this point, I stood up, and walked around the table to sit next to my son from foster care. Placing an arm around his shoulder, I continued. "If someone were to hit you with a stick, you might get a bruise for a few weeks. You might even get a broken bone. Those wounds will heal, though, after a time. But if someone were to call you a bad name, or say bad things about you, that can stick with you for the rest of your life, right?"

"I guess so," he said. I could see the light of understanding turn on in his eyes, as the anger that was there just a moment earlier began to disappear. "But, I can't help it," he added.

"Son, we are going to help you learn not to," I replied. "You are part of our family; an important part. We love you, and are happy you are here with us. We just can't allow you to talk like that to any of us. In our home, we don't say mean things, and we don't talk like that to each other, okay? If you do again, there are going to be consequences to your actions. Now, those consequences don't mean that we don't love you. In fact, we love you so much we are trying to help you be a better person. Do you think you can help us with this?"

Still looking at the table, the troubled nine-year-old wiped the tears that were beginning to form under his eyes. "Yes, sir," he replied. Giving him a hug, I then encouraged him to apologize to my own son. As he left the table in search of my son, I let out a sigh of relief and tried to release the tension and stress that had developed in my shoulders. I felt for Jimmy and understood that our rules were very strange for him. I also knew how difficult it was for him to abide by our family rules and was happy to be patient with him. Yet, this was just one incident of many, and I knew that it was going to take time and consistency from my wife and me.

I have found through the years that no two experiences in the foster care world are alike. This includes the experience of having a child from foster care placed into your home. In this situation, first impressions can make or break the child's transition into your home. After all, the first impression you create with your foster child is often vitally important to how the next few days and weeks will transpire. This will probably not be the sweet little child who rushes into your waiting arms, laughing delightfully, as you might imagine and may have hoped for. Instead, it is most likely that your foster child will be scared and frightened, full of anxiety. Along with this, he will also probably be confused, and may even be angry. To be sure, I have watched more than a few children placed into my home who were full of anger from being taken from their family and being placed in our home against their wishes. Your foster child may have left his family moments ago and is now told that you are his family, at least for the time being.

Without a doubt, he is full of questions as emotions swirl within him. No matter how much this child has been abused, whether it is physically or emotionally, your foster child will want their mother and father back. Despite the fact that you can provide a safer, cleaner, and healthier environment, he does not want to be there with you, but wants to be with those he was taken from. After all, these people have been the most important people in his life. Along with this, he has lost his familiar pattern of living, his home, his friends, and all that made up his own personal world. Although it is impossible to predict how he will react when he first meets you, it is important that you approach this time with caution and care, understanding and compassion.

The moment a foster child comes to live with your family and in your home, his whole world has changed completely. There are now different rules and different expectations to follow for him, rules and expectations that may seem very unfamiliar and very strange to him. Remember, your house is a new environment for him. There is even a set of new parents for him, and if you have children of your own, new brothers and sisters to get used to, as well. Everything he has known to be true from his previous home and biological family is now different. Make no mistake; these are significant and profound changes in your foster child's lifestyle. These sudden changes can be quite traumatic in his life and are sure to be very upsetting to him, as well. All decision-making has been taken away from your foster child, as he has had no say in being removed from his family, and placed into foster care. Indeed, your foster child is in your house against his will, and, in all likelihood, against his wishes. Quite simply, he doesn't want to be there, in your home, as everything is unfamiliar to him. It is not his family, it is not his home, and it is not his rules.

With this in mind, there is a good chance that any rules and expectations you have for your foster child will not be met. This is especially true in the first few days and weeks. This is a time to gain trust as well as simply get to know each other. It may take a while, but as a foster parent, you are in it for the long, tough haul. Make no mistake, is often times tough. For many foster children, they have been given up on numerous times. You just might be the first adults in their lives who will not give up on them. They may resist you and all that you have to offer. This is normal for a foster child. Remember, they may not want to be in your home, as it is not their own home. They may not want to be living with your family when they come to you, as it is not their own family. You could be the bad guy in this situation, and you can't expect them to embrace you and your family immediately, or even to like you.

To be sure, each child's placement is different. Some children in foster care may come to your house with a head full of lice and a body full of scabies, while some might be covered in dirt, and the few possessions they own, if any, carried in a black plastic bag. In fact, they may only have the clothes on their back, as several have when coming to my own home. Others may come to stay with you clean, healthy, and with a suitcase full of clothing, a box of possessions, and some money in their wallet. What is important is that you do not judge your foster child based on his arrival and appearance. However they arrive to your home, they will need your family's patience, your compassion, and your love.

T.J.'S STORY

My foster parenting experience can best be described as exciting and unpredictable. It was a learning process the entire time, specifically directed at the population with which we worked. First I worked with boys, then with girls, both victims and offenders, ages eight to 18.

The majority of my live-in time was with physically and sexually abused girls, mostly teens but a few younger ones. Severely abused, they had textbook behaviors such as fire setting, smearing, very low self-esteem, and scars in places people should not have scars. One of my younger girls, whom I will call Lisa, was 12 when I got her. Since she had no front teeth, I took her to a dentist. After examining Lisa, the dentist looked back at me and said, "Oh, she has front teeth all right. They have been knocked so far up into her gums, they are not visible."

Ironically, it was her older sister, who I will call Laura, who would really give us a run for our money with her issues. Laura had a habit of, about every 2-3 weeks, in the middle of the night, slicing her wrist just severe enough that it required one of us (family teachers) to take her to the ER to be assessed if she was safe from harming herself. Not once did they find it necessary to keep her overnight. What really made me curious was that Laura was always in a fine, bubbly mood at 3:30 in the morning on the ride back to the house. It was months later when we discovered what was so rewarding to her during these late night trips: attention!

We began to incorporate one-on-one attention time with staff during the day. Laura earned natural and logical rewards for participating in these times. Within a few weeks, her wrist problems went away.

Each individual had antecedents as to what caused their particular behavior. Almost every teen had a different outlet they used until all were taught to express their feelings appropriately. We called this process the ABCs. First came the Antecedent, which we had to identify, then the Behavior they showed, and finally, the Consequence they would earn. Usually the consequence was as natural and logical to the behavior as possible.

There was never a dull moment as a foster parent and some great feelings watching a teen doing things correctly for the first time and seeing the pride in their eyes.

Your foster child will need time to adjust to his new home and environment and will require time and patience from you. Along with this, he will also need your compassion, and your understanding during what is sure to be a very emotional and traumatic time for him. To him, everything is strange and new: a new home, new food, new family, and new rules and expectations for him to follow. Perhaps to compound his confusion even further, a new school, along with students and teachers, if he has moved from another school system. As you can imagine, it is likely that he may act out in a variety of ways as he struggles to understand the severe and sudden changes in his life. Your foster child may exhibit sudden outbursts of anger and aggressive behavior, extreme bouts of sadness and depression, or even imaginative stories about his birth family. Indeed, it is not unlikely that he will exhibit all of these. Furthermore, he may even express no emotions at all and seem completely shut off to you. As foster parents, it is important that you do not take his behavior personally. After all, he is attempting to understand his feelings and cope the best way he can, and perhaps the only way he knows.

The Power Of Our Words

Remember the old saying, "If you have nothing nice to say, don't say it at all." It rings just as true today as it did when you were a child. Even more so when it comes to children who have lived a life of abuse — they most likely have come from an environment where there was verbal abuse, as well. Then, there is the other old saying, "sticks and stones may break my bones, but names will never hurt me." A great saying that is taught to our children over and over, from one generation to the next and from one household to another.

Yet, it is a lie.

Through the years, I have seen the true power that words have. As a father to over 50 children from foster care over a decade now, I have had children come to live in my home who have never had a kind word said to them. Sadly, for them, profanity and harsh words were all they knew, words that were directed towards them on a daily basis.

We had a nine-year-old boy whose mother verbally abused him at every opportunity, calling him "a**hole" as her personal nickname for him. For the six months this boy lived with our family, he never had a kind word to say to another, he never smiled, never showed any indication of happiness.

The 17-year-old boy, who was homeless for 18 months, joined my family recently after being released from a county prison. When I asked him about his short time in prison, he commented that he liked being there, stating that "the prison guards were the first people who had treated him nicely."

We had a four-year-old boy who came to my home, and his every other word was one of profanity. This four-year-old boy even called my daughter the "n-word" when he first met her. A four-year-old boy! How does a four-year-old boy know this word? Perhaps it was from his grandfather who spoke like that on a consistent basis around him.

Sadly, these stories are not unique. Time after time, children come to my home, never hearing a kind word said to them. They were never complimented on schoolwork, how they looked, or for anything else. They were ever encouraged to try their best, and were never being told they were loved.

Words of affirmation, trust, and compassion are building blocks in the life of a child. Words of patience, kindness, and love are essential to the well-being, mental health, and emotional stability of each child.

Pick Your Battles

As a foster parent, you are most likely tired. There are some days when you feel exhausted, some days when we feel like we don't have the energy to do what we do. There are those moments when we struggle to maintain consistency, whether it is with routine, diet, house rules, etc. There are times when it is just too hard to face that child who is arguing with you on a non-stop basis.

Without a doubt, children want and need consistency in their lives, especially children in foster care who often had a chaotic life before coming to live with your family. Additionally, it is important that you maintain consistency in your home. Yet, we can wear ourselves out when we fight every battle, have the last word on every issue, and demand obedience at every moment. With this in mind, there are those times when we, as foster parents, can embrace the art of compromise and flexibility, especially when it comes to a child that argues constantly, fights you at every turn, and pushes the two of you in a daily power struggle. There are times when we need to "choose our battle," so to speak. As parents, we need to recognize that every battle does not have to be won by us, that every misbehavior doesn't need to be corrected. There are those times when we need to look for win-win solutions for both you and the child. We also need to understand that there are some house rules that can be flexible and some that must be maintained, at all times, for safety and wellbeing.

Time Out Vs. Time In

Time outs may be old-fashioned, but they still work today. Time outs can be used when a child is having an outburst of anger, for aggressive behavior, or for open defiance. When used properly, placing your child in time out allows him a few minutes alone and a few minutes away from an environment that was causing distress, resulting in behavior issues. Whether it is having him stand in the corner, sitting in a time out chair, sitting down on the bottom step of a staircase, or any other location you have decided upon, time outs can be an effective way of helping calm a child when used correctly. Ideally, the length of time a child remains in time out correlates with the age of the child: one minute per child's age. For example, if the child is four years of age, the child might sit in the time out chair for four minutes. If she is seven years old, she might stand in the corner for seven minutes.

"Time in" works differently from time out. Like time out, time in is another form of disciplining a child when issues of behavior occur. When a child is placed in time in, the child is placed into close proximity to you, the parent. Time in allows the child to be near you, or the adult, instead of away, as in time out. A time in may look like one of the following examples.

- A child sits next to the parent on a couch or chair, while the parent reads a book to the child or the two of them listen to soothing music together.

- A child sits across a table from the parent, and the two work on a puzzle together or play a game, while engaging in conversation.

- A child sits in a chair, stool, or even on a throw rug while the parent goes about with daily household chores. Perhaps the parent is folding laundry in a bedroom, cooking dinner in the kitchen, or cleaning the lounge room.

All three of these examples allow the child the feeling of comfort, safety, and security, as they are near the parent, instead of the feelings of isolation they may feel while in time out. Time ins may also encourage the child to open up and talk about their actions and their feelings while with the adult or caregiver.

Redirect

Redirection is a form of discipline that is becoming more popular in today's culture. Redirection allows a parent to guide and steer the child's misbehavior from one that is inappropriate to one that is more appropriate. When a child is redirected, it allows him to explore new opportunities, new experiences, and learn new skills.

For example, if a child is running up and down the stairs, in and out of your lounge room, and throughout your home, at full-speed and full-volume, you might have said, "Stop running and sit down!" You are frustrated, the child is frustrated and perhaps confused, and neither of you are at peace (well, perhaps you are a little at peace, now that the child is no longer racing through your home like an Indy race car). When you redirect a child, you might instead say "Sweetheart, I don't want you to fall down and get hurt when you run in the house. I think it might be better if you go outside and play. That sounds like a good idea!"

Rewarding Good Behavior

There are some who believe that rewarding good behavior is like bribing a child. I completely disagree with that statement. Indeed, my wife and I have been rewarding children in our home for a number of years, and have seen children grow, learn, and become much more responsible, as a result.

When a child is rewarded, he is receiving positive recognition for his efforts, his behavior, his successes, or his achievements. Quite simply, when you reward the child in your home for his behavior and successes, no matter how small, you are reinforcing his positive actions and encouraging him to do more of the same in the future. Perhaps it is a good grade on a report card, helping with the dishes, going a day without telling a lie, or eating his dinner without complaining to you about it; whatever the positive behavior or success, he needs to know, from you, that you recognize and appreciate it.

Now, a reward can come in a variety of different ways. If the child in your home picks up his room, maybe you could give him a high five, and say "Great job! I love it!" If she ate her veggies, an ice cream cone might be a tasty reward. If he completed his homework, maybe a brand new book might be an educational reward.

Loss Of Privileges

In our home, we talk a lot about consequences. For every action, there is a consequence, whether it is good or bad. It seems that today's youth are not being taught that there are consequences to both what they do and what they say. For those children who have come from homes and families that were abusive and neglectful, the idea of consequences may most likely be a foreign or strange one to them.

When a child behaves in a way that is not acceptable in your home, one form of disciplinary action on your part might be to take away or withhold a privilege. A privilege is something that we enjoy doing or having. For children, it might be staying up late on Friday nights to watch a movie, ice cream on Sundays, or going over to a friend's house. A privilege is different than a right. We all have the right to food, water, shelter, but I don't have the right to my favorite box of sugary cereal or watching my favorite movie over and over again. These are privileges. When a privilege is taken away from a child as a form of discipline, it helps to reinforce that the negative behavior or actions they engaged in were unacceptable.

Just recently, one of the children in my home had been repeatedly caught stealing food at the school's cafeteria. When I say repeatedly, I mean over and over and over again. My wife and I had discussed this with the child until we were, as you can guess, blue in the face. The school cafeteria manager, as well as the school principal, also had discussions with the child about it. We tried various forms of discipline, but none of them seemed to resonate with this particular child. One night, when we sat down together as a family for dinner, the little one who had been making these poor decisions at school did not get any homemade ice cream. She did not get the privilege of sharing in this tasty dessert as a consequence of her action. Now, my wife sat down the seven-year-old girl earlier in the afternoon, and told her beforehand that since she had stolen the food earlier in the day at school, that the consequence to this was no ice cream. I am most happy to report that she has not stolen any food from the school since that time. At least, none that I know of.

Professional Help

The truth is that there are times when you need professional help, and there should be no shame in that. Trained professional have a wide range of resources and tools to aid them as they help treat those who suffer with what might be ailing them, in whatever fashion that might be. When you have problems with a car, you see a mechanic. If you are building a new home, you might hire a carpenter. The pipes in your home aren't working right, so you call a plumber. Just like you go to a dentist when a tooth might be hurting or a doctor when you have the flu, trained professionals can help you with particular problems and difficulties you are facing. You contact or hire these trained professionals because they are just that: professional trained in a specific area and are experts in that field. The same applies for trained therapists and counselors. These experts have spent years studying and training to help in their field. As a foster parent, there will be times when you may have to call upon a professional therapist or counselor, and we will examine this further in the next chapter.

TOM'S STORY

"Six placements in two months," the worker said. She was talking about the two preschool siblings who had just come to live with us. That's not exactly what we were told. Rather, it was something along the lines of, "Well, they've been in a couple of shelters and one foster home. But that didn't work because of the fos-ter-mother's work schedule." But the reality was the children had regular fits of rage. I'm not talking about throwing a toy car across the room; I'm speaking of throwing themselves across the room, dropping in the middle of the floor and screaming at the top of their lungs for anywhere from five to 30 minutes at a time, dozens of times a day. I'm speaking of banging their heads against the wall re-peatedly until someone stopped them. The shelters asked them to be removed because they were keeping other children awake until 1 a.m. This is the world of the trauma-impacted child. These are children who have seen or been exposed to nightmares. So, how do you help a child like this? Can they be helped?

So what is the answer? At the risk of sounding overly trite, it's love. I'm not talking about the ooshy-gooshy, warm-fuzzy feeling. I mean genuine love, the kind of love that gives what is needed for the time at hand. Not an enabling act that simply allows the person to continue in unacceptable behavior as if to mistakenly think that the world revolves around them. I mean the kind of love that doesn't leave you abandoned. The kind of love that gives you what you need, not what you want.

We took our precious bundles of joy to the church Fall Festival amid hundreds of people. Didn't we know that there would be an explosion, before we went? Yes. Didn't we know that we would be VERY embarrassed by behaviors and that this was NOT going to be a Hallmark moment? Yes. So why go? Because that's what they needed. So we loaded up our other two small children and began our jour-ney. It was a tremendously fun time for the older kids. But, right on cue, one of the preschoolers threw himself to the floor right in the middle of that gathering and began screaming, kicking, and hitting his head on the floor. We got him to stop hitting his head, but otherwise remained calm. I'm sure that there was more than one indignant parent amid the crowd who wished we had kept our little ray of sunshine at home. But we didn't. And, once he saw that his fit didn't get him the attention he wanted, it only lasted a couple of minutes and he was done. He got up, finished our game, and went to the bounce house outside, where we repeated the cycle. "Wait! You mean you didn't punish him by taking him to the car?" Nope. "He still got to play other games?" Yep. And he had fun doing it.

These guys have been with us for about three weeks now and guess what? They go to bed on time, with very minimal fuss. They play around the house with one or two crying incidents a day, and for only about a minute in length. They clean up after themselves at playtime. And they even take naps during the day! They went from being kids that some would suggest need institutionalized to being functional little kids who still need direction and correction, but who thrive on praise. They LOVE to please. If you find a way to acknowledge the good they have done, you can visibly detect the swelling of their soul.

The children have got a long way to go. And, by the way, so do we. We don't get it right all the time. And it's easy to type out a success story that omits all of the stressful, agonizing moments of trying to figure out how best to handle a hurting child. But keeping that at the forefront is the key to loving them.

The Gift of Time

By now, you know that foster children face a very difficult time when being placed into your home. They have be taken from all they know and love, and instead have been moved to a place that is completely unfamiliar to them, a place that may frighten them and leaves them only with questions. This place of fear and uncertainty is your home. As safe, stable, and loving as your home may be, it is still the home of a stranger to your foster child. Without a doubt, he is going to need some time to adjust and get used to your home and your family.

With this in mind, the best gift you can give your foster child is the gift of time. To begin with, he will need time to grieve the loss of his family. After all, he has been taken from his mother and his father, his siblings and his relatives. He has been taken from his family. To be sure, he has been placed into foster care for a reason, and perhaps that reason is that his family was one that was abusive or neglectful. Perhaps his family beat him over and over again, abused him physically to within an inch of his life. Perhaps his family sexually abused him and emotionally scarred him. Yet, it is important to understand that this is his family, his norm. He loves his mother and his father, just as you love yours. As disturbing and as harmful as his home may have been, it is still his family.

He will need time, space, and understanding from you when he grieves for this loss in his life. Make no mistake, this is a major loss in his life, the loss of his family, and will likely be one that is quite traumatic. If he wishes to spend time alone in his room, allow him to do so. If he is quiet and withdrawn, do not push him to express himself and his feelings to you and your family right away. He may need this quiet time to reflect and process the many emotions that are surely swirling through him. If he breaks into tears and spends time crying, allow him to do so, and offer him a compassionate shoulder to cry upon, a warm and safe hug, and a listening ear from you. Remind him that there is no shame in crying, and that it okay to do so. After all, it is part of the healing process for him.

CHAPTER FOUR

Helping Children With Disorders

Imagine, if you will, being taken away from your mother and your father without any warning at all. Imagine being taken away from your siblings, your pets, your stuffed animals and toys. Imagine being taken away from your bedroom, house, yard, and neighborhood. Imagine, too, being taken from all of your relatives, friends, classmates, and everything you know. In addition, after all of this, imagine if you were suddenly thrust into a strange house, with strangers, and informed that this was your new home and new family for the time being. How might you feel? I can bet that you would be scared. I know I would be. For thousands upon thousands of children each year, this is not a figment of their imagination; this is a reality that is full of questions, full of fears, and full of trauma.

Being placed into your home, a foster home, is a distressing, harrowing, and life changing experience for a foster child. Placement disruption is the term used when a child is removed from a home and placed into the custody of a child welfare agency, and thus into a foster home. For many, it is a frightening time, as the fear of the unknown can quickly overwhelm a child. Others are filled with anger, as they emotionally reject the idea of being separated from their family members. Feelings of guilt may also arise within the foster child, as the child may believe that he or she may have had something to do with the separation from the birth and/or foster family. Some children experience self-doubt, as they feel that they simply did not deserve to stay with their family. For all, it is a traumatic experience that will forever alter the lives of foster children.

CATHI'S STORY

I knew as soon as I met Jamie that this was going to be a difficult placement. The eight-year-old girl had been heavily sexually abused by her father before she was placed in our house. She called me "Mommy" and my husband "Daddy" when we first met her. That was my first red flag that something wasn't exactly right. Normally, the kids that were placed in our house were afraid of my husband and me, and were scared to be at our house. Of course, I understood why; these kids didn't know us. We were perfect strangers to them, and they missed their own mommys and daddys. Jamie didn't act that way, at all. She seemed almost excited to be with us.

The second red flag came later that night, when we went to church for Wednesday Night Service. Jamie was very happy to be going and had a huge smile on her face as we got in the car. As soon as we walked into the church dining hall, Jamie ran up to a stranger and gave him a hug. You can bet that this stranger, who was a good friend of ours, was a little surprised, but he gave her a hug back, anyways. Later that night, after dinner was over, Jamie went over to another stranger, and sat in his lap while we were all listening to the preacher. Before I could get out of my chair and get Jamie, our newest foster daughter had snuggled up close to the stranger, and he looked very uncomfortable. It was as if she didn't know a stranger, and that no one had ever told her about "stranger danger." My husband leaned over to me and said, "I think we have a problem. This isn't normal."

—Cathi

Many psychologists state that it is necessary for young children to form a relationship with at least one main parental figure or caregiver in order for the child to develop socially and emotionally. Yet, the removal of a child from his or her home, and the subsequent placement into another's home through foster care, often makes this difficult, traumatic experience. Often, the removal of a child from a home occurs after a caseworker has gathered evidence and presented this evidence to a court, along with the recommendation that the child be removed. Indeed, most foster care placements are made through the court system.

As distressing as this may be for a child, even more traumatic may be the removal from the child's birth home comes without any notification. These emergency removals oftentimes occur late in the evening and with little to no warning for the children. As caseworkers remove a child from a home suddenly, most are unprepared. Foster children leave their home with a quick goodbye, leaving behind most of their belongings, with some clothing and perhaps a prized possession hurriedly stuffed into a plastic bag. Before they know it, they are standing in front of you, strangers, people they have never met before. Against their will, they are in a strange home, their new home. With most children in foster care, it is a time of fear, a time of uncertainty, a time where even the bravest of children become scared. Indeed, foster children often have no control over this transition, no control where they are placed, and no control of when they will go back to their birth family. It is this lack of control that many times sends children in foster care spiraling into depression, various behavioral issues, and a world of anxiety.

Many times, children placed into foster care suffer from mental health issues. A placement disruption may be so severe to the child that it feels as if their entire world is falling apart. For them, it is. Everything they know to be true in their world is now turned upside down. Their mother and father are no longer there to comfort them when they are troubled or afraid. The family they lived with, grew up with, laughed with, and cried with is no longer there to take care of them. The bed they woke up in each morning is now different. Far too many foster children, the school they went to, the teachers they learned from, and the friends they had formed relationships with have also been taken from them. These children now live with a strange family, wake each morning in a different house, sit in an unfamiliar classroom, and are no longer surrounded by those who love and know them best. Children in foster care often struggle to best deal with and survive these traumatic events, as they struggle to adjust to a new home and new family. To be sure, the losses in their life, along with the lack of a permanent home, often times prevent these children from forming a secure and healthy attachment with a primary caregiver.

Issues from anxiety can manifest themselves in a number of ways. Perhaps the one that foster children face the most is separation anxiety, an excessive concern that brought on by the separation from their home, family, and to those they are attached to the most. Indeed, the more a child is moved, from home to home, from foster placement to another foster placement, or multiple displacements, the bigger the concern becomes. Those children who undergo many multiple displacements often create walls to separate themselves in an attempt to not let others into their lives. In doing so, many foster children end up lying to their foster families as they try to keep their new family at a distance, and at the same time, give the child a sense of personal control.

Other anxiety disorders include *obsessive-compulsive disorder*, where a child repeats unwanted thoughts, actions, and/or behaviors out of a feeling of need. *Panic disorders* find a child experiencing intense bouts of fear for reasons that may not be apparent. These attacks may be sudden, and unexpected, as well as repetitive in nature. Panic disorders also may coincide with strong physical symptoms, such as shortness of breath, dizziness, throbbing heart beats, or chest pains. Another anxiety disorder that foster children may face includes *social phobias*, or the fear of being embarrassed or face the criticism of others.

Dealing with separation and loss is difficult for anybody. As an adult, you have likely had experience with this, and know who and where to reach out to when in need of help. Children on the other hand, generally do not know how to handle these feelings and emotions. Yet, these feelings must be released in some fashion. One way of expressing these feelings of isolation is to lash out in anger and frustration to those around them. Though foster children do not necessarily blame you, the foster parent, or the caseworker, the feelings of frustration and loss are strong within them, and you may be the only one they can release them to. Anger may also result in destruction of property or items within your foster home, as the child lashes out.

Post Traumatic Stress Disorder (PTSD)

ASHLEY' STORY

Recently, I was caring for a sibling group of three children, ages 13, 14, and 15, who had all suffered horrible, horrible abuse. The 14-year-old girl was pregnant with her father's baby and truly thought it was normal. The father took the children away from their mother while one was still a newborn and the others were only one and two years old. He started having sex with her when she was four years old. The kids were not allowed to have friends and couldn't talk to anyone on the school bus. They were made to share their school breakfast with their father. They weren't allowed to have their picture taken at school. The two boys had Ricketts, a softening and weakening of bones in children, and were wheelchair bound. Many therapists said they could walk, but the father forced them to keep their wheelchairs so he could get the disability money. He then began pimping out the girl to help with finances. He withdrew her from school so she could do that.

Eventually they were removed. She had the baby, and he was privately adopted. She was in and out of facilities for about a year or so. Child Welfare was going to put her in a hotel because no one would take her in. I stepped up and offered to help because she trusted me. When she came into foster care, she was confused and everyone kept telling her that her dad was evil and needed to be put away, but that wasn't what she needed to hear. I began visiting her once or twice a week just to talk to her about anything and everything. When she would talk about her dad, I would simply listen instead of giving judgments. Eventually, a few months later, she opened up to me and admitted that the father of her baby was her own father and began discussing the abuse. No matter what facility she ended up in or how many foster homes she went to, I would always check on her and make sure she knew I was around and that I would never give up on her. I think that solidified her trust the most.

She suffers from many things, and Post Traumatic Stress Disorder is one of them. She's been hospitalized once since she's been in my home but otherwise is doing much better. She struggles with her emotions and gets overwhelmed and irritated easily. She doesn't like big groups of people. She sometimes has a hard time with logic and reality. The oldest brother is now 19 and still in care. He is in an Independent Living Program (a program designed to assist youth in foster care achieve self suffiency,) apartment and doing OK. The youngest brother is in a foster home. He's 16 now. Even though he's been in the same foster home, he has had many violent outbursts and problems in school.

—Ashley

Post Traumatic Stress Disorder, commonly known as PTSD, is a psychiatric disorder that occurs when someone has witnessed a traumatic event, such as the death of a loved one, a natural disaster, a severe accident, or a form of abuse, whether it is mental, physical, or sexual in nature. Those who suffer from this disorder often have re-occurring nightmares, thoughts, feelings, and memories of the traumatic event or incident, and may even relive the event over and over again in flashbacks. Additionally, those who suffer from PTSD also have feelings of anger, depression, fear, or sadness, and may withdraw or become detached from others. Some other symptoms in children may include overly aggressive behavior, drug and alcohol abuse, sexual behavior, and self-harming behaviors. Finally, those with this disorder will often try to avoid any situation or environment that might remind them of them of the traumatic time. For some children, though, they may instead try to keep repeating a part of the traumatic event through a game or through play, as the memory of the event continues to play over in their mind. PTSD may appear in the person weeks, months, or perhaps even years after the traumatic event initially occurred. Indeed, it is often not diagnosed in a child until well after the incident took place.

One study from the Child Psychiatry and Human Development magazine found that those children in foster care between the ages of six and eight, one out of every three suffered from Post-Traumatic Stress Disorder. Another study, from Harvard Crimson, found that children in foster care suffer from Post-Traumatic Stress Disorder at twice the rate of American war veterans. To be sure, we often hear about PTSD in our war veterans, and rightfully so. Yet, we seldom hear about it among children in foster care. Why might that be? Well, my suspicion is that children in foster care are often overlooked by society and the media, as are the problems facing them. Thus, it is just one more reason why you need to be an advocate for the child.

I am a big believer in the power of play to heal. Play therapy is a form of therapy, or treatment if you will, that is most commonly used with children between the ages of three and eight. This therapeutic method allows the child to freely and naturally express himself through the simple act of play. It allows the child to cope with the emotional traumas, anxieties, and stress he is facing through an act they are familiar with. I have taken many children living in my home to these play therapy sessions, which generally last about 45 minutes to an hour, and have found this type of therapy to be most helpful with children who not only suffer from PTSD, but with other anxiety- and trauma-based disorders, as well. To be sure, these play therapies are important to a child's healing and treatment, as the trained therapists are able to not only monitor and observe the child's actions, but also help treat the child, as well.

Eye Movement Desensitization and Reprocessing (EDMR), is another form of therapy where trained therapists use the child's own rapid, rhythmic eye movement instead of a talk session to help the child deal with the traumatic events in their lives. EMDR therapy helps facilitate the accessing of the traumatic memory event, as information is processed while enhancing new associations between the traumatic memory or event and more adaptive memories or information. Cognitive-Behavior Therapy (CBT) is another form of therapeutic treatment in which trained therapists teach children how to recognize their thought patterns and how to use problem solving skills to help themselves.

Now, you might not be a trained therapist and might not have access to all the latest therapy treatments, but there are ways you can help a child in your home who suffers from PTSD. To begin with, you can help reassure the child that they are indeed safe and in a safe environment with you and your family. Remind the child repeatedly and consistently that the traumatic event that he experienced is now over and that you will keep him safe. Along with this, allow the child plenty of opportunities in which he can share with you about what happened and how he feels about it. To be sure, this should be done only when and if he feels comfortable doing so, with no pressure from you to do so.

Routine is another way to help children deal with anxiety in their lives. Children need and thrive upon routine and consistency in their lives, and as you know, children placed into foster care seldom have come from such environments. Be consistent with how you respond to the child when he misbehaves, acts out, or withdraws because of his anxiety and distress. Finally, you can have a little play therapy session of your own in your home. Allow him opportunities to color, draw, play, and develop the power of imagination. In other words, give him the chance to play. Make no mistake, you might have to sit down and color with him or get down on the floor and play dolls with her. You might have to teach the child in your house how to play. Yes, teach her **how** to play, as she may have suffered so much abuse that she has forgotten how to do that, or lived in an environment where she never learned. Show the child in your home that it is okay to laugh.

Disinhibited Social Engagement Disorder (DSED)

I have had many children come through my home who, as Cathi put it earlier in this chapter, "didn't know a stranger." There was the four-year-old girl who gave a hug and a kiss to every man she met. One year, we had a seven-year-old who did the same. Then, there was the little boy who was overly talkative to every person he met, on every occasion. For several months, we cared for an 11-year-old who sought a hug from my wife and me at every opportunity, and would do the same from her teachers at school, those at our church, and anyone she met. These children all had Disinhibited Social Engagement Disorder, or DSED.

Disinhibited Social Engagement Disorder is a childhood attachment disorder where a child will actively approach someone they are unfamiliar with in an attempt to interact with them. DSED may develop in a child due to a lack of a nurturing or affection from a caring adult or caregiver early in his life. As a result of never truly developing a healthy, affectionate, and loving relationship or bond with a parent or adult, the child seeks to find it in others and is as comfortable with a complete stranger as they are with his primary caregiver. Children who suffer from DSED are often very talkative and social with strangers and have no fear giving a stranger a hug or a kiss. There is no sense of "stranger danger" in a child who has DSED. As the child grows into an adult, the symptoms of DSED seem to diminish.

Treatment for Disinhibited Social Engagement Disorder is often found in professional therapy sessions with trained therapists. Many times, you and your family may be asked to attend a family therapy session with the child. There is no need to feel alarmed or uncomfortable about this. My wife and I have attended several such therapy sessions with a child in our home, and I have found them to be both helpful and very interesting. In fact, I have come away from many such sessions having learnt some things myself. Additionally, play therapy and art therapy are often used when treating children with DSED. Art therapy is fast becoming a popular form of therapy that combines psychotherapy techniques and practices with art. This form of therapy allows the child to express themselves through coloring, painting, sculpture, or through other forms of art, allowing them to communicate their feelings when they may not be able to do so verbally. For myself, I have had several kids come to live with me who did not have the verbal skills to express themselves, either because they were quite young, were never taught such skills, or had suffered so much anxiety that they had withdrawn from others.

KAY'S STORY

Loud screams woke me from my sleep. I stumbled from my bed, rubbing tired eyes as I fixed a bottle of formula. I picked up my foster son from his crib, gave him the bottle, and went to the rocking chair. I patted him as I rocked, but he didn't melt into me, like most babies would.

Carson was not like most babies. He had been in three different homes by the time he was 7 months old. He was wary and watchful. He didn't lean into me when I rocked him, and he screamed night after night. I watched him drain the bottle, and then the dreaded screaming began. What do you do when there are six sleeping people in a small double-wide home? There was nowhere to go, nothing to do.

I rocked and patted, humming softly to Carson as he flailed and screamed. For months, this was our routine. He screamed until he couldn't stay awake. I couldn't bear him screaming alone in his bed, so I held him.

I prayed over him, oh, how I prayed! I loved him, cared for him, and yet he screamed.

I wondered if it was alcohol. His mother claimed she didn't drink when she was pregnant, but was she telling the truth?

I wondered if it was the insecurity of being shifted between so many homes from birth. That has to do something to a baby.

I wondered if I was crazy to even think I could be a foster parent? What was I thinking? I was not equipped to do this! I was a miserable failure! These doubts crept into my mind while I was rocking him in the middle of the night.

My tears ran down my face and joined his, in those dark hours of the night. I wept and prayed and wept some more. Sometimes I wasn't sure if I wept more for him or me. His feelings of being lost broke me. My brokenness drove me to my knees. I was no longer a rescuer of kids but one who desperately needed rescuing from my own selfishness.

I wanted sleep! Just sleep! But as he cried night after night, I knew my loss was temporary, his was forever. Therefore, I could put my needs aside for his. For one more night, by the grace of God.

Reactive Attachment Disorder (RAD)

Perhaps one of the most common disorders that children in foster care often face is Reactive Attachment Disorder, otherwise known as RAD. As I work with foster parents across the globe, I often hear of the challenges they face when caring for children who suffer from RAD, children who are unable to form or develop a healthy relationship and an emotional attachment with a parent or caregiver. Like with Disinhibited Social Engagement

Disorder, this lack of an emotional attachment may result from abuse or serve and extreme neglect. As a result of the abuse and neglect early in their lives, children who suffer from RAD are especially distrustful of others. Additionally, when angered or frustrated, these children are very difficult to calm down, due to the feeling of the lack or loss of control they are feeling. Even more so, children with RAD are often withdrawn, sad, and melancholy.

Other symptoms of Reactive Attachment Disorder include a lack of affection from the child, and even a lack of response when you try to show affection to the child. Along with this, those with RAD have difficulty looking someone in the eye, as well as interacting with others. Finally, children with RAD are often unexplainably irritable or angry and often difficult to soothe when in such a mood.

REBECCA'S STORY

I am a former foster child who decided to repay the kindness that was shown to me. We went to our local Social Services office to fill out paperwork and left with six- and 10-year-old girls. It was like God had brought them in at the exact time that we would be able to help them. My husband and I have two children of our own, ages four and six. The six-year-old foster child had RAD. She had a hard time finding her place in the family. She was hitting and taking things that didn't belong to her. She was smearing her stool and hiding underwear in her bedroom daily. We considered more than once having her moved, but I felt it wasn't in her best interest to do so. So we persevered. After about four months she was still very jealous of our three-year-old. One day she was in the basement and our little one found a toy that she hadn't been able to find in a while and was very excited about it. The foster daughter was very jealous and kicked her in the face, cutting her mouth and causing it to bleed. At that point, I sat her in a place away from the other kids and called the child welfare worker on call. She talked me out of having her moved and offered added supports for the girl, including intensive in home therapy. That is when we saw a big change in her. All four girls really started bonding and still call each other sister. We pray daily for the children in our area.

—Rebecca

As you can imagine, professional therapy sessions and therapists are essential when trying to help and treat children with Reactive Attachment Disorder. Additionally, you can help a child with RAD by being nurturing, caring, and consistent with your responses to him. Along with this, try to provide a stimulating environment for him in your home; one that will give him plenty of option and opportunities to learn from and be nurtured by. As you can imagine, having a child in your home who suffers from RAD will be exhausting, and at times, frustrating. Therefore, your patience is absolutely essential. Make sure your expectations of the child are reasonable and realistic. Don't expect treatment and therapy to quickly resolve all issues, and don't expect that simply loving the child through this process will relieve all of his symptoms. Instead, celebrate any success he might have with his behavior, however small that success might be. Try to find moments where the two of you can laugh with each other, and try to cultivate a feeling of joy in your home. Most likely, as you well know, he has come from a home where there was little laughter and little joy.

Attention-Deficit/Hyperactivity Disorder (ADHD)

It may come as no surprise to you what studies from the American Academy of Pediatrics have found: children in foster care are three times more likely than others to be diagnosed with Attention-Deficit/Hyperactivity Disorder.

Attention-Deficit/Hyperactivity Disorder, commonly known as ADHD, is a medical condition in which brain activity and brain development are affected. While ADHD is highly a genetic disorder, it can also result from alcohol and tobacco consumption by the mother during pregnancy, as well as from high levels of exposure to lead and even pesticides. The disorder may also run in the family, so to speak, as it can be a condition that is diagnosed in both parent and child of the same family. Additionally, ADHD may also result from a significant head injury.

Children who suffer from Attention-Deficit/Hyperactivity Disorder have considerable difficulty concentrating and focusing on tasks that demand their full attention. Along with this, they also struggle with listening, and often daydream, or shift their attention and focus to other issues, instead of upon the task before them. This may result in a child seeming forgetful, inattentive, or even absentminded, at times.

Along with this, Attention-Deficit/Hyperactivity Disorder also may result in a child acting rashly or in an impulsive manner. Their emotional reactions may seem overly dramatic or intense in a situation that you may feel does not warrant such a reaction. Furthermore, they may interrupt others and may find it difficult to wait until it is their turn in the task before them or when talking to others. These children may rush to do things, without seeking permission and without thinking their actions through. Children with ADHD also seem restless or hyperactive, and may become bored more easily than others. They may struggle with sitting still or keeping quiet, and may disrupt others around them in doing so.

Attention-Deficit/Hyperactivity Disorder has no known cure, yet the disorder can be treated in many different ways. First, those who have ADHD may benefit from medications that are designed to treat the disorder. These include both stimulants and non-stimulants, and your doctor can tell you what medication will best treat the child. Along with this, behavior therapy is also another way of treating someone who suffers from ADHD. Research shows that behavior therapy is an important part of treatment for children with ADHD. This type of therapy helps to reduce the behavior issues that affect a child with ADHD while at home, in the classroom, and other environments. Along with this, behavior therapy also strengthens and reinforces positive behavior. Other forms of treatment are psychotherapy, as well as family therapy

Fetal Alcohol Spectrum Disorders (FASD)

I have had so many babies, infants, and children come join my family who have suffered from Fetal Alcohol Spectrum Disorders, otherwise known as FASD. In fact, some have joined my family permanently, through adoption. I am sure you have probably come across children with FASD at some point in your life, as well.

Fetal Alcohol Spectrum Disorders are a collection of conditions resulting from a woman consuming alcohol while pregnant. The alcohol consumed by the mother passes through the umbilical cord and into the baby in the mother's womb. It is as if the baby itself is drinking alcohol. FASD can contribute to a number of challenges, both physically and with behavior and learning. In truth, children born with FASD often have a combination of both issues.

There are a variety of symptoms in regards to Fetal Alcohol Spectrum Disorders. They include a height that is shorter than average, low body weight, and smaller head size. Babies often have abnormal facial features, including a smooth ridge between the upper lip and the nose. Children with FASD also have great difficult in school, most often with reading and math, due to poor memory ability, learning disabilities, speech and language delays, and simple difficulty with attention. Additional symptoms include poor powers of judgment and reasoning, problems with hearing and vision, and even heart and kidney complications.

There are four main types of Fetal Alcohol Spectrum Disorders. Perhaps the one most people are familiar with is Fetal Alcohol Syndrome, or FAS. Children with FAS often have complications with growth and facial feature abnormalities. They also have difficulty with attention span, communication, learning, and memory, and more than likely will struggle in school in some fashion. Another form of FASD is Alcohol-Related Birth Defects, or ARBD. Those born with ARBD have health related issues with hearing, heart, kidney, or even with bone. Children diagnosed with Alcohol-Related Neurodevelopmental Disorder, or ARND, have learning and intellectual disabilities and struggle in school. Finally, Neurobehavioral Disorder Associated with Prenatal Alcohol Exposure, or ND-PAE, is a disorder in which children struggle with behavior problems, mood swings, and attention, as well as have trouble with basic living skills. Children diagnosed with ND-PAE also have thinking and memory difficulties, too. As noted in an earlier paragraph, it is common for children with FASD to suffer from a combination of these four disorders.

Tragically, Fetal Alcohol Spectrum Disorder is a condition that the child in your home will not grow out of once he reaches adulthood. Indeed, FASD is a lifelong condition. Fortunately, there are a number of ways FASD can be successfully treated. Early diagnosis is vital and essential in order to best help and treat someone who suffers from FASD. There are several types of medication and medical care for those with FASD. Additionally, you as a foster parent can help the child in your home who suffers from FASD by seeking out special educational programs that are designed to meet the needs of the child. As we have learned, children with FASD struggle with a combination of learning challenges. He needs you to help him survive and succeed in school with these special educational programs. Do some research on your own and reach out to your school system or local social service programs. Finally, like mentioned in this chapter several times, a consistent, loving, nurturing and stable house and family will truly help the child.

TISH'S STORY

My fourth placement came to me June of 2015. I was told he would likely be long-term, even likely to come up for adoption, as there was no appropriate family to care for him. He was one of five siblings. His biological father had taken the other four children who were his and not the biological mother's, and ran once CPS got involved with my little guy. At one point he even asked for a DNA test and claimed my little guy wasn't his. He never worked services and never contacted CPS or had visits until the very end of the case. My little guy was brought to me after he was removed from a family friend who had abused him. He was taken to that family friend because he was removed from mom and dad. Little man was meth positive, and when I say positive, his numbers were extremely high. Not only was it suspected that meth was being smoked in his presence, but also that it was being manufactured and sold in his home. Mom had a history of meth use and manufacturing, as she lost her daughter a few years prior for some of the same reasons. She had also committed an attempted armed robbery and stolen a vehicle when she lost her daughter. At the time my little guy came into care, Mom was on parole. She was then put back in prison because my guy being meth positive was a violation of her parole.

The meth exposure caused a number of developmental delays in this baby. He was two years and three months old when he came to live with me. He was placed in speech, occupational, and behavioral therapy with ECI, but he had such severe issues, especially behavioral, that those therapies were not enough to make improvements. Thinking that I should be super foster mom and find out what is really going on with this baby and the best way to help him, I searched out a psychological evaluation because I thought he was autistic. He made very little eye contact, had no empathy for others, was extremely aggressive, and strong for his size and age. I had him evaluated, and he was diagnosed with Reactive Attachment Disorder, not autism. He also had sensory processing issues. In the evaluation, the psychologist stated that he should remain with me so as to learn how to form proper attachments and bonds. I then sought out therapies for both him and my first placement that would help improve some of the issues they were having. Placement number one had been with me more than two years at this point and was also diagnosed with sensory processing, emotional disturbance disorder, and adjustment disorders. Placement number one was also evaluated, and I was told he needed physical therapy to help with his poor motor skills.

I sought out a therapy called listening therapy, in which the children listened to music through a headset while they completed occupational therapy tasks. The music was especially tailored to each child and their specific needs. This therapy was at a facility that was a three-hour drive each way, once a week. Here again, I thought I was doing something great and was being super foster mom.

I had to endure extreme aggression with placement number four, not just towards me, but towards placement number one and animals. There was a time when his aggression got to a point I had to rehome one of the dogs just to protect the dog. Placement number four would get placement number one to turn against me, and both would gang up on me and violently attack me to the point I had to lock myself in a room, and all I could do was cry. When these aggressive moods would happen, I'd have to remove one of them from my house and have the aggressor stay with my mother. Again this wasn't good in CPS' eyes either, as they felt I was using my mother's home as a way of punishing the children when they became aggressive. The recommendation to separate them came from the boys' therapist. This same child also had no impulse control, was nearly kicked out of daycare for violence against other children, and for laughing at punishments or laughing when he hurt others. He had no empathy. All this being said, he could also be the sweetest most loving little boy, and he was very attached to me. When I would leave him, he'd stand in the window and cry, watching for me to come back.

When he first came to me, he called everyone mom. After a few months, he only saw me as mom. I had made many improvements with him. He used to run out into traffic and scare me to death, but with the therapy I was getting for him all that improved and everyone saw that.

Even though placement number four was a drain on me in so many ways, I loved him so very much. He went back to live with his biological grandma originally and is now back with his biological father. Even writing this now brings me to tears. I still love and miss him every single day, and it's been 19 months since I lost him. Not a day goes by that I don't think about him or look to see if I can find a Facebook post or photo of him. He was my little Superman. He made me weaker at one point, but in the end stronger.

CHAPTER FIVE

A Foster Parent's Broken Heart

My tears flowed freely down my face. My cheeks were wet, yet I wasn't compelled to wipe the tears away. Quite simply, my heart hurt. My heart was broken.

It had been two months since Maddie, our last foster child, had left our home. The four-year-old girl had been with us for just under one year and had made a significant impact, not only on both my wife and I, but on our own children, as well. She had very much become a part of our family, and there were talks about the possibility of adopting her. Sadly, as it is many times for foster parents, the four-year-old was moved to another home, where she would be closer to her biological family members. It was an emotionally difficult time for us. Her last words to me stung deep, "Daddy, will you miss me when I am gone? Will you still love me when I leave?"

Two months later, it still hurt; I still cried.

"Will you still love me when I leave?"

I wanted to find her, to reach out to her, and to tell her, "Yes, Maddie. I will still love you. I will always love you."

Now, this may be something you don't want to hear, but foster parenting is supposed to be hard in this area, this area of grief and loss. You see, it shouldn't get any easier for you when a child leaves your home, and leaves your family. You shouldn't get too used to the feeling of missing a child when he leaves your home. In fact, this is really how it should be, right? We should grieve for the child when she leaves. We should cry when we miss him. This is okay, and this is healthy. After all, when our heart breaks for a child that we have cared for in our home, it means that we have really cared for that child in a way that he needs. This means we gave him what he needed, truly needed, from us. Of course, children in foster care need stability, they need security, yet what they truly need is for someone to love them with all their hearts, so that when they do leave our home and our family, our hearts break. Your broken heart, your feelings of grief and loss, mean that you have been able to develop a healthy, loving attachment and relationship, or bond, with that child, a bond he needed. So, it is okay to hurt. In truth, children in foster care need us, need you and me, to hurt for them, need us to feel deep sadness, need us to experience strong feelings of loss. Sadly, we might be the only adult or parental figure in their life who did love them unconditionally.

Saying goodbye is never easy for anyone and may be especially difficult for you and your foster child. After your foster child leaves your home, you may feel like you never wish to foster again, as the pain is too great. The grief you feel may be overwhelming. Please remember this though, my friend; you are not alone. It is normal for foster parents to feel loss and grief each time a child leaves a home. Take time to grieve, and remind yourself that you are not in control of the situation. And please remember this: it is okay to cry as a foster parent. It means that you gave the child what she needed the most: someone to love her with all your heart.

RANDY'S STORY

I woke up from the dream in an agitated state. Sweat was dripping down the side of my face, despite the fact that the fan was on overhead. It was the same recurring dream I had had several times the past two months: my four-year-old daughter from foster care, Ashley, and I were holding hands and laughing.

A happy dream, to be sure, under normal circumstances. This was not so happy, though, as the four-year-old child was no longer living with me.

I missed her terribly.

Later that afternoon, my wife mentioned that she had had a similar dream the night before about Ashely, as well. My wife had not stopped grieving the loss of little Ashley from our home, as her tears had been flowing freely, both in home and in public.

Ashely came to live with us a year ago, a victim of severe neglect as well as horrific sexual abuse from a biological family member of hers. When she arrived at our home, the frightened girl's vocabulary was not only limited, she could not speak a word, only grunting and pointing. Her eating and toilet skills were also negligible, and it was as if we had an infant in our home. Now, after nearly a year in our home, the four-year-old was speaking in sentences, eating healthy, and more importantly, laughing and smiling.

Due to regulations and policies from the child welfare agency in our state revolving around the fact that she was one of four siblings, little Ashley was placed in another home. Days leading to her moving from our home to her new one, Ashley would ask my wife and me, "Mommy and Daddy, will you cry when I leave?" That question alone opened up the tear ducts in both my wife and myself.

Now, Ashley was gone, hopefully living with her forever family, a family that would adopt her and her siblings. I tried to find joy in this fact, as we were simply unable to adopt her and her other siblings, for a variety of reasons. To be sure, adoption was no stranger to us, as we had adopted three of our own children from the foster care system. Yet, Ashley was unique. Ashley was different. All who met the little one were captivated by her smile, under the spell of her laughter, and she was loved by all she met.

Ashely was our daughter, as are all of the children from foster care who come to live with us. On this morning, I was once again grappling with the heartache that gripped my heart since Ashley left. The pain I felt at times was too much to bear, leaving me in tears.

I didn't know if I could continue on anymore. I didn't know if I could continue to be a foster parent; continue to have my heart ripped out when a child left; continue to wear myself down, exhausted at each day's end. I didn't know if I had the strength in me anymore to care for children in need in my home and with my family.

—Randy

For so many foster parents, the hardest part of caring for children in need in your house is the day they leave your home and the day they leave your family. So many times for me, the removal of the child from my home has come with little warning and with great emotion. As a foster parent, your home becomes a place where foster children come for a period of time, with the goal of being reunited with their family in the near future. Now, as you no doubt know, reunification is not always possible for some foster children, as the birth parents' rights are terminated. As a result, these children become available for adoption, and some foster parents do indeed end up making their foster child a permanent addition to their family through adoption. For my wife and me, we have had the wonderful opportunity to expand our family by three, with the adoption of three children that were our former foster children.

On the other hand, if reunification should not become possible with the birth parents, many foster children instead are placed into a birth family member's home. This might be a grandparent, an aunt or uncle, or even an older brother or sister. Whatever the reason might be, reunification can be a difficult time for foster parents, as the child they have come to love leaves their home. At the same time, it can also be a time of great celebration, as the biological family members are able to now properly care for and raise their child, and a family is whole again.

As I noted earlier, through my own experience, there are times when the removal of a foster child from your home may come suddenly and without any prior warning. You might get a surprising phone call one afternoon, informing you that the child in your home is to leave the following day. Indeed, it has happened to me on more than one occasion, leaving me with a head full of questions. This may be due to a court order, health reasons, or placement into another foster home. Other times, plenty of notice is given to the foster parents beforehand, giving both the child and your family ample time to prepare for the child's departure from your home and from your family.

Now, before I was a foster parent, I did not understand the heartbreak that children in foster care truly suffer from. Nor did I understand the heartbreak that you and I, as foster parents, go through as well. You may have heard this story from me in person at a speaking engagement or from some of my previous writings. Yet, I want to share with you here, as this my personal story that drives me each day to help other foster parents, as well as all children in care.

Sydney was only seven years of age and basically taking care of herself when she joined our family upon being placed into foster care. Living with her severely alcoholic grandmother, the little girl had to find and prepare her own food each morning and evening, usually consisting of frozen hot dogs warmed in the microwave. Along with this, the parentless child, whose mother and father were both missing, was also responsible for getting herself ready for school each day.

As a result, she often missed catching the bus each morning and had a large amount of absences, resulting in her performing at a severely poor level, academically. When the seven-year-old arrived in our home, she had very few academic skills, so much so that she could not even write her own name. Her behavior in school was also a challenge, often resulting in meeting with the school principal and myself.

Though Sydney's stay in our home was one filled with many challenges, she had become a valued member of our family during the year and a half she lived with us. She was our daughter, and we loved her. There was no difference between our biological children and Sydney; no labels. All were loved the same.

Then, two days before Christmas one year, Sydney left our home and family and moved to a nearby state, as her aunt and uncle had adopted her. I had great reservations and concern regarding this, as she had only met the couple one time beforehand. Despite my many pleas to the caseworker to have the young child to stay with our family until after Christmas, Sydney instead went to live with the family she hardly knew, spending a Christmas with strangers instead of a family she had lived with and who had loved her for nearly 20 months. It was a time of much sadness and tears in our home, as we all grieved the loss of this special child in our home.

Whenever you are told, there will sure to be emotions involved, for both you and the foster child. The removal of a child may be a joyous event as you celebrate the reunification with the child's birth family, or one that is filled with grief, as you are filled not only with heartbreak, but with grave concerns about the child's future wellbeing. If the removal of your foster child is one that you disapprove of, due to his new placement, it is important that you do not share these feelings with your foster child. If you must express your concerns and feelings with the caseworker, do so in private, as it will only serve to burden the child with more anxiety during this difficult time of separation.

Each foster child is different and each placement into a home creates different sets of emotions. As a foster parent, there may be those children you do not have strong attachments to, due to emotional or behavioral issues, yet an attachment with these children is still made. Some foster children will be so difficult that you may even ask for them to be removed. Still, other foster children will steal your heart and will become a dear and cherished member of your family, leaving you heartbroken. When any foster child leaves your home, no matter the level of attachment, there will be emotions when it is time to say goodbye, for both you and the child. Rest assured, many foster parents do feel grief during the removal of their foster child, as the child has come to be an important and loved member of their family. After all, the removal of a foster child from a foster home is akin to a loss, and any loss can cause grieving.

BEV'S STORY

The hardest thing I ever did was the day Julie left my home.

Little Julie was our foster daughter for a year and a half. When my husband and I got a phone call from our caseworker, asking if we could take the one-year-old, the two of us prayed about it, and then called the caseworker back, telling her that we could. Little did I know that our whole lives would change and that our hearts would be broken 18 months later.

Julie had been abused by her stepfather and neglected by her birth mother for her first year of life. The little one came to us weighing next to nothing, with bruises on her arms, her back, and her face, all beatings by her stepfather. She could not look us in the eye and made very little sound, not even normal baby talk for her age. The doctor told us that she would probably have learning disorders when she got into school, along with speech and language development problems. The therapist told us she might also suffer from attachment issues because of the heavy abuse and neglect her little body had to endure during her short time alive.

Almost immediately, our whole family fell in love with our little angel from foster care. My own five-year-old daughter and seven-year- old son wanted to know if they could be Julie's big sister and big brother, and of course my husband and I happily said yes. Our two biological children soon helped feed and care for Julie, as well as play with her. After a few months, Julie began to gain the weight she desperately needed, and even began laughing. What a miracle it was to hear her laugh, after all the pain and suffering she had gone through earlier in her life.

Yes, there were hard times. All the doctor appointments for Julie, all the hearings with the caseworker and the court, and all the missed meetings at visitation times with her birth mother and other biological family, like the grandmother and the aunt, who all hardly shown up for the visitations. It was all worth it, though, and when one day our caseworker told us that the mother's rights to Julie might be terminated, we began to hope for adoption.

One afternoon, my husband got a call from the caseworker, telling him that Julie was going to live with her grandmother, despite the fact that the grandmother had rarely visited our foster daughter during the time she lived with us. We had two weeks to say goodbye to our beloved angel. It was hard on my husband and very hard on our own two children. We had to explain to them that Julie was going to live with her grandmother and had to assure my own kids that Julie would be safe, that she would be okay. Both my husband and I weren't so sure of that, but we prayed for the best for our little angel. For me, it was heartbreaking, and to this day, a year later, I still haven't gotten over it. I miss her, terribly. I miss how my own kids would hold her. I miss her hugs, and I miss her sweet laughter and smile.

—Bev

Just like Bev, it is important to understand that anytime a loved member of our family leaves our home feelings of grief and sadness are normal for foster parents. There are also those times when we may become angry, frustrated, and upset over the removal of a child from our home, and placed into another home, perhaps that of the birth family. As a foster parent, my friend, it is necessary for you that you remember this: you are not in charge of the situation. The court system very often makes the decision to have a child removed from a home, including yours. There have been times that I have disagreed with this decision and have even engaged in spirited conversation, if you will, with my caseworker regarding this decision. Yet, I need to remember, as you do, that we are usually powerless when this happens, and our voices and opinions sometimes go unheard, or so it seems.

If you are a studier of psychology, then you may know that grief is something personal and different for each of us. Some will cry, like my wife, while others hold it inside, like I sometimes do. Others will immerse themselves in a job, a task, or something else, to try and escape the pain they feel, while still others may become detached from others, and even sink into depression. When a child from foster care leaves your home and your family, it can be emotionally devastating, for you, and for all involved. Let's take a look at the stages of grief, as I described in the book *The Foster Parenting Manual*,[1] based on Kubler-Ross, and how they may affect you, as a foster parent, when a child leaves your home.

Stage 1: Shock

The removal of the foster child may bring feelings of shock to the foster family. After a family member has formed an emotional attachment to the family, the sudden removal may cause deep shock and uncertainty, leaving the foster family confused.

---

1. DeGarmo, 2013

Stage 2: Denial

With a sudden departure, some foster parents may deny that they ever formed a relationship with their foster child or feel any sadness towards the removal. Even though they deny these feelings, they grieve, believing that they were unable to provide the help the child needed.

Stage 3: Anger

A foster child's removal from a foster parent's home may bring feelings of anger and severe disappointment with the caseworker, as well as with the child welfare agency system. Foster parents may blame the system or caseworker for the placement of their foster child into an environment they feel is not productive, or even harmful, to the child.

Stage 4: Guilt

During this stage, foster parents may experience feelings of guilt, blaming themselves with the belief that they are at fault. They try to comprehend what they did "wrong" that caused the removal of the foster child. Still, other foster parents may experience guilt if they were the ones asking for the removal, as they were unable to continue caring for the child.

Stage 5: Bargaining

Some foster parents will try to substitute the grief they have by helping others in need, in an attempt to justify the loss of their foster child. Other will try to substitute the loss with the placement of another foster child in their home, hoping that this new placement will help them forget about the child that just left.

Stage 6: Depression

There are different components to depression brought on by grief. Some foster parents will become easily irritated and others will experience a constant state of feeling tired. Others will feel as if they can no longer continue with their day-to-day lives and have a difficult time with the tasks associated with family, friends, work, and marriage.

Stage 7: Acceptance

After the passage of time, the grief from the loss of the foster child decreases, allowing the foster parent to accept the removal of the child and move on. The emotional well-being of the foster parent improves and a sense of understanding of the child's removal becomes clearer.

Yet, it is not just foster parents that grieve. The biological children of foster families also grieve.

RACHEL'S STORY

I am a biological child of foster parents. My siblings and I, who spanned in age from eight to 14 years old, were fascinated with the idea of foster care.

Nothing could prepare me for the reality of the two little sisters who arrived at our door. The toddler had eyes of wonder and confusion. Though she was wary of my parents, she warmed up quickly to my siblings and me as we brought her toys and played with her. That worked out well because my parents were busy with her infant sister. The baby was suffering the effects of drug withdrawal. She would tremor, break out into sweats, squirm, scream, and bat away her pacifier. She needed to be given regular doses of morphine just to deal with the pain of the withdrawals.

Though my parents did not share all of the details of the girls' case, my parents would prepare me for changes that might happen. As the girls began more visits with their birth parents, my parents told me that the social workers were looking to move the girls back with their parents soon. Before the girls came back from difficult visits, my parents would remind my siblings and me that the girls might act out because of the tough stuff they had to deal with. As time passed, various relatives dropped out of the girls' lives and the parents were unable to make positive progress. After a rocky month, the county asked if our family would be willing to adopt the girls.

Although my parents prefaced this new revelation with caution and "this is only an option; this is not for sure at all," my heart was dancing in the possibility. These girls, my sisters forever? Yes, please! The more I looked at it, the more I thought it was perfect. We knew the girls' likes, dislikes, and fun personalities better than anyone. They had lived with us for a year. The baby, now perfectly healthy and walking, had her first birthday with us. Her sister was my little sidekick.

One evening, two days before Christmas, we got a call. With only hours of warning, my family had to pack up all of the girls' belongings. A social worker arrived in the morning and took them to one of their relatives to live.

With one call, my sisters were gone. My parents tried to make it an enjoyable holiday season, but we were all grieving. Because the social workers had observed the bond between us biological children and the girls, my parents asked if we could send the girls cards or pictures we had drawn. My parents asked if our family could call the girls once they were settled. We wanted the girls to know that we had not abandoned them. In the end, the social workers did not allow any contact. Nor did the county have any resources to recommend when my parents asked for advice for helping biological children when foster children left.

The grief was lonely. Not many people understood what we were going through. Even within our family, each of us coped differently.

—Rachel

To be sure, it is hard being a foster parent, and it is hard for all who live with and care for children placed into foster care. The grief when a child leaves can, at times, be overwhelming and all-consuming. It is like losing a child, a member of your family. Yet, I don't want you to give up when a child leaves because your heart is heavy. There are other children out there, right now, who need a home and need a family. There is a child out there right now who needs you to love him.

CHAPTER SIX

Looking After Your Marriage

There are days when the joys and successes of foster parenting can be rewarding and exhilarating. There are also those days when the disappointments and frustrations can be challenging. To be sure, these disappointment and frustrations as a foster parent can be difficult and even damaging to a marriage. Sadly, I have known more than one marriage that has broken up over issues related to foster care. To be sure, many marriages can feel the strain due to foster care related issues and stresses. My wife and I have felt the strain of having multiple children in our home with a variety of traumas, traumas that have placed our own household under stress and strain. It can be challenging to a marriage, and it can be draining.

Just recently, my wife and I were caring for another round of 11 children in our home. Three were biological; three were adopted from foster care; and the remaining five were from foster care, a sibling group of two and another sibling group of three. Now, let me be clear, please. My wife and I do not have a group home, nor are we superheroes of any kind. It was simply that both sets of siblings needed to be placed that day, there was an emergency, and no other foster homes in the area were available. Thus, with some prayer and discussion, my wife and I agreed to the larger household — and the impending lack of sleep that was sure to come our way.

Was it difficult? Absolutely! Suddenly, we had seven children in our home in diapers each night. That was difficult enough. There was unending laundry, cooking, cleaning, bathing, and child care, and it was exhausting. Add to that our older children who were in the school's marching band, along with their homework each night. And then there were the committees and meetings that my wife and I raced to and from in the evenings after work, along with the other responsibilities we had with work, church, and so forth. Yet, the addition of the various forms of traumas that the children from foster care brought into our home was perhaps the most difficult part. It seemed as if each evening was spent trying to comfort a screaming child, a child suffering from the emotional scars and traumas inflicted upon him before entering our home. My wife and I struggled with not only trying to comfort and care for these children, but for all the children in our home. Quite simply, there was not enough time in the day to do all that we needed to do. By the time we got to bed each night, we had scarcely said three words to each other all day long. We were exhausted, tired, and worn out by the end of each day. Not only did our own line of communication suffer as a result, but the strains and additional workload left us both too tired to spend any time with each other. As you can imagine, exhaustion led to frustration at times.

Indeed, there are a number of ways a marriage can face times of stress and strain while children from foster care are placed into the home. Here are some ways that your own marriage can be hurt while being a foster parent.

TINA'S STORY

My husband and I had been foster parents for four years. When we first started, we both wanted to help children. We had been married for seven years and had found out that we were unable to have children. We thought that being a foster parent to a child who needed a family was the next best option. We both wanted kids and had so much to offer as loving parents.

Our last placement was particularly hard on my husband. He had come to really love the little five-year-old boy in our home, and we had both hoped to adopt him. Unfortunately for us, our little one went back to his mother, after living with our family for 14 months. It was hard on me, but it was crushing on my husband. I believe he is in a state of depression, as a result.

I am ready to have another child come live with us, even if we can't adopt. We didn't set out to be foster parents just so we could adopt. We just wanted to have the opportunity to have kids in our home, to help raise them, and to love those who especially needed a loving family. My husband is not ready to foster again, and says he might never be able to do it. It hurts to watch him this way, and I want to take his pain away. At the same time, I want to be a foster parent again, and want to have the chance to love a child in my home. When I talk to him about it, he gets upset. It is hurting our relationship and hurting our marriage.

—Tina

A Marriage Neglected

You and I both know this to be true: being a foster parent can take a great deal of time and energy from you. When you are looking after a child from foster care 24 hours a day, every day, every week, every month, it can be time-consuming and leave little time for you and your spouse or partner. At the same time, if you are like me, your marriage to your spouse is vitally important to you. After all, you married your spouse for a reason right? You wanted to spend the rest of your life with that person, the person who makes you laugh, who supports you in good times and bad, who cares for you, and who you love with all your heart. Now, when you both agree to be foster parents, you will certainly make sacrifices in your life, as you surely well know. One of those sacrifices is the gift of time with your loved one. It can be easy to neglect a marriage when you are caring for a child in need and a child that demands all your attention.

What About Yourself?

Yes, you are busy, busy, busy. The lifestyle of a foster parent. When you are indeed caring for children in need in your home and family, and doing so constantly, not only might you neglect your marriage, you can also neglect yourself. Hobbies, interests, personal space, friendships, and time alone often disappear altogether when being a foster parent. You lose sight of who you are, you burn out and become worn down, causing a possible strain on your marriage.

Sleep? What's That?

People often ask me when I sleep after they hear of my busy schedule, day in and day out. I often tell them that I will sleep either next year — or when I die. Sleep is something that you and I often go without, and certainly don't get enough of, would you agree? When we have those children living with our families that require a great deal of care and supervision, it can be both time-consuming and exhausting. The crying child who misses her birth parents; the angry child who is screaming at you once again; the child whose medical needs are not being properly met can wear you and your spouse out. Plus, there is the constant supervision of the children, the homework, laundry, cooking, cleaning, visitations, doctor appointments, court appearances, meetings with case workers, and on and on. When do you have time to sleep?

Discipline Disagreements

You and your spouse or partner might have a difference of opinion on how to discipline the child in your home. When these disagreements occur, it can cause a serious strain on a marriage.

I was at a foster parent conference awhile back, delivering a keynote address on the importance of foster parenting. After the speech was over, I was approached by a young couple, probably in their mid-20s. As they approached me, I could see the look of discouragement on both their faces. Coming to the table I was at, their heads were bent down and hushed whispers escaped from both their lips. After a few words of greetings, they told me their story. The couple was in the third year of their marriage, and they were unable to have children of their own biologically. They were in the midst of their first placement of a foster child in their home: a nine-year-old boy who had come from severe physical abuse. The young boy had been very defiant towards the couple, refusing to follow their instructions. On top of that, he had shown aggressive behavior towards the pet dog in the house. Not wishing to give up on the foster child and have him re-moved, the couple wanted to continue to try and work with him. What they struggled with was the way they should discipline him for his behavior. The husband wanted to withhold many of his privileges and "ground him," so to speak. The wife, on the other hand, wanted to be more lenient in her discipline. As you might have guessed, this was causing some angst in their young marriage and bringing additional stress to the household. This couple is not alone, I assure you, with issues such as this, as many marriages are under stress when trying to come to an understanding of how to best discipline a child, whether it is a foster child or a biological child.

Oh, The Money

You have heard the whispers, and perhaps even the false accusations, that foster parents are in it for the money. These people couldn't be further from the truth, right? We both know this to be true: it can be financially straining and even stressful when taking care of foster children. There are those times when the needs of our children from foster care can be rather expensive, causing further strain on our financial well-being. To be sure, foster parents are reimbursed for many things. Yet, if you are like me, my wife and I spend a great deal of our own money on the children when they come into our home. Food, additional clothing, soccer games, music competitions, gas in the car as we run the children to and from visitations, doctor's appointments and other activities. Along with that, there are birthdays, holidays, and other special events. To be sure, many agencies do give foster parents some financial assistance with these events. Yet, many times, this type of aid, or reimbursement, does not cover the costs of making a birthday, holiday, or a special event just that: special. These all add up, and place a strain on our own wallets. That can surely bring discussions of money between you and your spouse, discussions that can add even more stress.

The Stress of Working with Biological Parents

Throughout the years, as I have cared for children in my home and family, there have been those times when I have been cursed at, had objects thrown at me, spat upon, and even lied about in court. On one incident, a biological parent followed my wife home in the car. I imagine you might have some similar stories. It is important for us to remember that in the eyes of some biological parents, we are the bad guys, the ones who took their children away. Foster parents represent a part of their lives that they may not want to remember or even refuse to acknowledge. To be sure, there are those times when working with biological parents can be stressful, for all involved. Maybe you disagree with their parenting styles. Maybe their morals and values differ completely from you. Maybe they have said mean things to you or about you. Even if they have committed unspeakable abuse against the children, we are not to judge them. Even if they have abandoned the children, we are to work with them. Even if they have been rude and mean spirited against us, we are to remain patient with them. Is it hard? To be sure! Is it frustrating at times? Without a doubt!

Disagreements

It happens with my wife and myself. I imagine it happens to you and your spouse from time to time, as well: martial disagreements. In every marriage, like any partnership, there are going to be disagreements of some kind or another, at some point in time. After all, if you are married, have a partner, or are living with another adult, you are bound to argue at some point about some issue. Whether it is about the discipline of a child, financial situations, child rearing, work-related issues, or even about the in-laws, you will not agree with your spouse on everything. And guess what? That's okay. It doesn't mean your marriage is falling apart. After all, you married somebody who has different views on certain things. Yet, when you are fostering children in your home, the stress of taking care of children in need may add an additional pressure to those disagreements. Sometimes, these disagreements may lead to bigger arguments between you and your partner, thus brining an even great level of anxiety and stress to your relationship together.

Resentment

From time to time, I hear stories from foster parents who have struggled with issues and feelings of resentment towards a child placed in their home, and even of feelings of resentment towards their partner and spouse. One particular story was from a foster father, and how he and his wife disagreed about having a teenager placed in their home. The troubled teen often had issues of behavior and was frequently in trouble at school, as well. Additionally, he was openly defiant towards the foster father, adding even more stress. While the foster father was ready to have the child removed from the home, his wife did not wish to do so, as she felt she would be "giving up" on the teen. As you probably guessed, their relationship and marriage was under extreme stress over their disagreement about the continued placement of the teen in their home. Furthermore, the foster father was developing feelings of resentment towards the child, and sadly, towards his wife, as well.

I am afraid that something like this almost happened to my family. We had a child placed in our home that was so very needy, so very draining, and very exhausting. Our 11-year-old foster daughter had suffered from sexual abuse and neglect for several years. To be sure, our hearts went out to her, and we tried to help her in every way we could. Yet, she had suffered so many traumas in her young life; she was incredibly needy and did not know how to socially interact with others in a healthy fashion. She would knock on the door while my wife or I were in a shower asking for hugs, on a daily basis. She would also often walk into the bathroom while my own daughters were showering, asking for hugs as well. The poor girl would cling to my wife or me as if she were glued to our sides. She would also interrupt anyone in the house who might be speaking and had a very difficult time with the truth. It came to the point where my own children resented having her in our home. This resentment by our own children caused a tremendous stress within our family and household, and even led to our children wishing that we weren't a foster family any more.

The Stress of Saying Goodbye

As we saw in the last chapter, foster parents experience feelings of grief and loss when a child leaves the home and the family. You have come to love this child as a dear and treasured member of your family. Yet, when a child moves out, whether due to the wonderful opportunity that reunification can bring between a child and his family. Additionally, stress may be added when a child leaves your home to be adopted by another loving family, or, perhaps the child has become a young adult and aged out of the system, and out of your home. Whatever the reason might be, when a child from foster care leaves your home, it can be very emotional and can lead to depression and anxiety on your behalf. To be sure, when we as foster parents experience such feelings, additional stress can be added to our marriage.

It is very clear to see that caring for children in foster care in your home and in your family is not only stressful to you, it can also be stressful to your marriage. What I often emphasize to those couples who are foster parents is that their marriage and their relationship comes first. After all, you don't want to have your marriage and relationship end because of foster parenting. Hopefully, you will remain married to your loved one long after you stop being foster parents.

So, how do we address these challenges? What do we do to help with these particular stresses? How can we best strengthen our marriage while we are foster parents? Well, let's look at a few ideas.

Making Time for Your Marriage

I am so very blessed, on so many levels, to be married to my wife, Dr. Kelly DeGarmo. She is the light of my life, and I am such a better person because of her. I recognize that I married far above my position. There is no doubt that I could never do all that I do without her support and her strength. We both work hard to make our marriage as perfect as it can be, and we both work hard to support each other in all we do.

Every marriage, every relationship, needs both partners to put work into it, if the relationship is to be a healthy one. How does that happen? Well it will be absolutely necessary that you spend some alone time with your partner as often as you can. Yes, this can be hard, and it is something that my wife and I struggle with at times, as well. Yet there are ways to do this. A great way to do that is to have a date night once a week, or once a month.

Go see a movie, go out to dinner, go shopping together. If you are like my wife and I, and a whole evening is simply not possible, even small moments matter. Try to have a quick lunch together, have a joint prayer and meditation time, or walk around the neighborhood one evening. Just make sure you do something together that involves only you and your partner, with no children involved. I am talking a child-free span of time, my friend. This time alone is important, as you can share your concerns, desires, hopes, and wants, not only as a foster parent, but as a married couple. It is important and essential that you have one-on-one time with your spouse, your partner, and your best friend, if you wish to make your marriage a healthy and strong one. If you do not make this a priority, your marriage will suffer and perhaps even come to an end.

Time for YOU!

We addressed some of this earlier in Chapter 2. You need to take time for yourself.

For the first time in about nine months, I was able to get outside and do some work in the yard. I have been a lifelong gardener, and I often found refuge while gardening: it was time for myself to reflect, think, and relax. Of late, I had neglected my gardening chores, due in large part to having nine children in the home. I was not making time for the garden, and thus not taking time for myself. As a result, I was becoming worn out, exhausted, and was approaching a burnout that I did not want or need.

As I tackled the job of pruning back the many butterfly bushes in my yard, I felt the stresses and tension that had been in my shoulders the past months quickly slip away. Indeed, it had been a difficult time the past six months, with a house full of children. The latest children in foster care in our home had come with a variety of challenges and needs that were all too demanding of my wife and me. We had both grieved when the two youngest foster children were placed into another home, a home with no children where the foster parents could completely focus on their many needs. With nine children in our home, my wife and I were spending all our time trying to meet the needs of these two, while almost ignoring the other seven. Perhaps it was best for all of us if these two were placed into another home that could give them all the support and resources they needed. The oldest foster child stayed with us, a decision that the courts, the case workers, and the teen all felt was best, and one that we so very wanted as well.

Pruning back the branches and spent flowers from the previous season, I allowed myself the first opportunity in a long time to take some time for myself, to do something I enjoyed. I needed this time alone, and I could tell right away that I would be better for it, and my family would benefit from it, as well. In an almost humorous light, I laughed to myself, thinking that seven children seemed much easier than nine. Foster parents certainly have a different perspective of things in life.

I know of some people who become so engrossed in being a parent and taking care of children that their own personal identity disappears over time. Don't neglect who you are and what makes you special. After all, your spouse fell in love with you for who you are! When foster parenting becomes too stressful, you, your family, and your foster child will all feel the effects. Thus, one of the most important reminders for you, as a foster parent, is the fact that you need to take care of yourself, physically, mentally, and emotionally. If you neglect yourself, your family will suffer as a result. Finding time for you will not be easy, but it is very essential. Make time to do something you enjoy, and that you find relaxing. Spend time with some friends, perhaps over lunch or dinner. Do not neglect your own personal health: make sure you exercise regularly and eat healthy. If you take time for yourself, you will help to ensure your well-being, as you care for others in your own home. Oh, and that includes sleep, as well!

Help From Your Own Family

As we have seen, you will need the full support and commitment from your partner and spouse when you are caring for children from foster care in your home. Along with this, you will also need the full commitment and support of your own children. We will examine this further in Chapter 7, but before we do that, it is important to note right here and now that the support and commitment of your own biological children is essential. If not, your own marriage will suffer.

Fortunately, our own children once again became somewhat of a lifesaver for my wife and me. With the extra laundry, cooking, cleaning, bathing, and other household chores that came along with a large family, my wife and I would have been quickly overwhelmed by it all after a hard day at our day jobs. It was the help of our children that eased this load. Our children were invaluable to us, whether it was changing diapers, feeding babies, doing dishes, and even reading bedtime stories. If for at one moment our children rebelled at the thought of having more children in foster care placed in our home, my wife and I would have had a much more difficult time of it.

In Agreement

The children in your home are watching you and your spouse. You are, after all, an example of what a healthy marriage and healthy relationship looks like. If it looks like to the child that the two of you are not in agreement with decision making, then chances are that you are not in agreement. Looks are not deceiving in this area, my friend. The two of you need to work to be in agreement with each other. When it comes to issues of child rearing, discipline, and other issues that relate to foster parenting, it is necessary that you and your spouse are in agreement with these issues. Be willing to be flexible and overlook small and minor disagreements.

The Communication Factor

Maria, a veteran foster parent, recently told me that she and her husband make time to talk to each other every day. The two do this late at night, sitting at the dining room table with a cup of coffee after all the kids have gone to bed. The two talk about the challenges before them, schedules and appointments, future plans, and the personal struggles they might be experiencing.

Maria and her husband are right. Communication is so important to a strong marriage. Many marriage experts will tell you that it is the key tool for a happy and successful marriage. You and your spouse need to make sure that the lines of communication are freely used and completely honest between the two of you. Be honest with her about what is bothering you and bringing you stress. Tell him about the doubts or concerns you might be feeling and experiencing. Share with your loved one what's on your mind and in your heart. If you are on the listening end, make sure you listen with an open mind and with your full attention. If something is bothering you, share this concern with your loved one. When your spouse is sharing their concerns with you, be sure to listen; simply listen.

So, when your spouse or partner come to you with a question, concern, even if he just wants to talk, turn the television off, power down the computer, and put the phone on silent and in your pocket, look them in the eye and just listen. This will go a long way to not only strengthen your marriage and relationship, but to bring the two of you closer together.

United and Together

There will be those children who will test you and your spouse. They want to see if the two of you are in agreement together on things like bed time, homework, socializing with their friends, online devices and social media, and discipline. Some children want to see if the two of you are together in your parenting, or if they can play one against the other. When it comes to issues of child rearing, discipline, and other issues that relate to our foster parenting, it is necessary that you and your spouse try to be in agreement with these issues. Additionally, there will be those times when you need to recognize that the two of you can be flexible on some issues.

Along with this, do not take your foster child's behaviors personally. Keep in mind that his behavior is a learned one, probably from the environment that he came from previously. Your foster child is behaving the way he was taught to before he came to live with you. It will likely take some time and effort to change his misbehavior, poor habits, and disruptive manners. Indeed, you may never be able to completely curb him from this type of negative behavior. Again, do not take this personally, as these learned traits may be deeply ingrained within him and were reinforced by his previous home for a long period of time, even years. Do not let his behaviors affect you and your marriage. You were married before the child came to you, and your marriage should last after he leaves you. The child is placed in your home for a temporary time. Hopefully, your marriage will last a lifetime.

How "NO" Can Strengthen Your Marriage

Time and time again, I hear from foster parents who tell me that they have a very hard time saying "no" when the phone call comes for a placement in their home. They just find it hard to say "no," perhaps out of guilt, perhaps from the fact that they are afraid that if they say "no," another phone call might not come. I can relate. My wife and I had a hard time with this for several years, as well. It seemed that we said "yes" to every call that came our ways, despite the fact that sometimes we were just too tired and worn out to do much more.

By now, I hope you recognize that there are times in your foster parenting life when it is okay to say "no." It is okay to take a break and focus on yourself, your children, and your marriage. There are times when we are just too busy that we can't even begin to think about tomorrow because there is so much to do today. At this point, we no longer become helpful to the child who needs our help. My friend, it is important for you to recognize those times when you can't take anything else on because you have enough to handle and take care of at the moment. If you don't recognize those moments and times when "no" is the right word at that particular moment, you will bring additional stress upon yourself, your family, and your marriage. Learn the art of saying "no" so that you don't overburden, overstress, and overextend both yourself and your marriage.

A World of Resources and Support

We live in a world where we can learn just about anything at the click of a button from our own personal digital devices. Laptops, computers, tablets, phone; we now have the ability to research on anything at any time. For me, as a lifelong learner, I love this! I am always researching something every day; whatever sparks my interest at that particular moment, I look it up on my computer and learn all I want to know about it.

For foster parents, this is a wonderful resource to have available. There is an eruption of information being released about foster care, parenting, child-care, and trauma online every day. As foster parents, we now have more resources and information accessible to us than ever before. Indeed, when I first became a foster parent so many years ago, there was very little material to read. That's why I started writing many of my books like this one; I wanted to help you and other foster parents navigate this new lifestyle. Now we have websites, social media pages, articles, and other resources available to us. To be sure, this is incredibly helpful, as it allows us to read and learn about a number of issues that we face as foster parents and that affect the children living in our homes and families today. I remember recently when I had a child placed in my home with a condition that I was unfamiliar with. That first night, after he went to bed, I went downstairs to my library and got online to do some researching. By the time I went to bed, I was more knowledgeable about his condition and better prepared to help him when he woke up the next morning. You can do the same. As you go online and gather information and resources about all things foster care, you become a stronger, more prepared foster parent, and thus help to strengthen your marriage, as well. After all, knowledge is power, right? The more knowledge you have, the stronger you will be come as a foster parent, and the stronger you will become in your marriage, as well.

As we saw earlier, it is important to have your own support group to lean on as well. This applies not only for your personal life, but also as foster parents. A support group of fellow foster parents can also help strengthen your marriage. As you find strength and wisdom from your foster parent support group, whether in a local foster parent association, through an online social media group, or through both, you will find that some of your stress and anxieties that come from being a foster parent to a child in need will ease. This will, no doubt, help your marriage, as well.

The Power Of Respite

My wife and I recently took our first real vacation together, with no children, in over 20 years. Let me share that again with you. We took our first real vacation, as a couple, just her and I, child-free, in over 20 years. While it was only for a week, it was an incredible rewarding and enjoyable time, as we were able to reconnect with friends of ours from Europe. When you are in an international marriage like mine, you end up having friends from every part of the world? A part of me didn't want to come back home, as it had been a refreshing, much-needed break for the two of us. We were able to do so, in part, because of respite care.

There are those times, of course, when foster families simply become exhausted, or "burned out," if you will. Perhaps the foster child has been in the home for an extended period of time, and the family has grown mentally, emotionally, and physically weary from care. To be sure, this is a very real possibility, and is one that should not be ignored. In order for the family to remain not only healthy foster parents, but a healthy family unit, they may merely need a break from care, an opportunity to "recharge their batteries" and focus on their own family unit, lest it begin to suffer from exhaustion and lack of attention. Respite may be the solution. Respite is a resource for foster parents that allows for the child to be placed into another foster home for a brief and temporary amount of time while the original foster family regains some of their strength. Most often, the child remains in the same school system during his time in respite, and with a foster family that lives in the same general area as you. If your marriage is under strain, and you feel like you can't continue much further, you might wish to consider this respite as a way of recharging your batteries. We shall examine respite care further in Chapter 9.

My friend, your marriage and your relationship to your spouse or partner is so very important. It's even important to me! You need to take steps to not only maintain your marriage and relationship, but also to strengthen it. Of course, this is important when you are both caring for children in foster care in your family and when you are not. In other words, you need to focus and work on your marriage at all times. So, let the new honeymoon between the two of you begin!

CHAPTER SEVEN

Your Own Children and Family

My biological children are a very important part of my foster parenting. Without them, my wife and I would not have been able to foster the 40-plus children that have come through our home. As you know by now, we have a large number of kids in our house at the same time, up to 11 on a few occasions. You should see my car when I go to church on Sundays. It is like a clown car: children keep coming out, and coming out, and coming out of it. Without a doubt, the stares follow us everywhere we go. We are a like a travelling circus!

For the longest time, we averaged about nine children in the house. As you can imagine, with such a large number of kids, and very active kids at that, the house can become quite dirty, quite quickly! The amount of laundry, dishes, and general cleaning needed can become overwhelming in a hurry. Along with those responsibilities are the soccer games, homework, dance lessons, marching band practices, piano lessons, and other activities that children are involved in after school. Furthermore, there are doctor's appointments, therapy sessions, and visitations that come along with children in foster care. At the end of the day, my wife and I were often exhausted, worn out, beat, and just plain tired. With such a large number of kids in the house, we have far exceeded the Brady Bunch in terms of children. Yet, we have no Alice; we have no maid nor help. It is just my wife and me taking care of all these children on a daily basis.

So, how do we do it? Quite simply, we rely on our own children from time to time. If not for the help of our children, the workload might have crushed us. Not only did the children help out with the laundry, dishes, and other household chores, they also helped with feeding our many younger foster children, reading them stories, and playing with them. Most importantly, though, our own biological and adopted children have come to love their siblings from foster care, and treat them as part of our own family. It is this love that has been an instrumental part in how our foster children not only fit into our home and family, but has also been vital to helping the healing process that many of our foster children have sorely needed. It is this type of help, and this type of love that has helped us to continue to be a foster family, despite the difficult times and challenges we have faced over the years.

CHARONNE'S STORY

When we made the decision to begin the process to become licensed foster parents, our biological children were quite young. Our oldest son was six years old and our youngest was just two years old. We included them in the decision-making and preparations as much as we could, but they had no idea what our family was really in for.

From the moment we got our first placement call, our boys were overjoyed! They welcomed this tiny girl, unknown to them, as a sister. In fact my biological children have gained three "siblings" in the short time we have been involved in foster care.

Our biological children have experienced great gain and joy through our involvement in foster care, but they also have experienced loss. We welcomed another foster placement, a second "sister," who was more challenging for them to connect with. She was a terribly hurt and scarred little girl and our boys spent months trying, giving up, and trying again before they could connect with her. I will never forget the night the breakthrough came and this sweet, hurting little girl began chasing our youngest son around the house giggling and smiling ear to ear. That is a picture I always will keep in my mind and my heart.

A few months later, this second "sister" transitioned out of our home. We did everything we could to make this a smooth transition for everyone involved. We threw a goodbye party, made a special box of remembrances from her time with us, and put together a photo album for her. Every member of the family made a picture or a letter to send her off. We even went to Build-a-Bear Workshop® and made her and our three other children each a matching bear. Each of those bears is filled with four hearts, filled with love from "siblings" that were together for just a little while, but will be together forever in their hearts.

Since our second foster daughter left, we have welcomed in our first foster son. Our biological sons were ecstatic when they learned a "brother" was joining us this time.

Recently, we had the opportunity to tie ribbons around trees in Milwaukee County to help promote awareness of the need for foster parents. Our boys came along and excitingly joined in spreading the word about foster care. It filled my heart with joy watching their arms stretch around those big trees to tie a ribbon with big smiles, knowing the good our family is doing.

—Charonne

To be sure, I have changed as a person in so many ways as a foster parent and am a better person for it. At the same time, my own children have changed, as well. Now, as we both know, the life of a foster parent is one of sacrifices, in so many areas and in so many ways. The same is true for the life of a foster sibling for your own biological children. For my own children, this life of sacrifice has transformed my own children into my heroes. My children have been fantastic as foster siblings to the many children that have come to live in our family. Not only have they helped out in so many ways, they have learned to share their clothes, their toys and books, their food, their bikes, their love, and most importantly, their parents. They are more patient with others their own age, whether it is in our home, at school, or on the playground. They are more understanding of children their age when others might act out in some fashion. My children have learned the art of compassion and personal sacrifice. They have seen the best and the worst in others. They have learned the important lesson of what consequences can be had from making poor decisions in life. My children are more loving people, care more about society and the world around them, and are more sensitive to the needs of others.

LAURA'S STORY

My own nine-year-old son watched a video "Camp" on a boy entering foster care, and he instantly showed us how big his heart is. He said any boy in our home could take some of his Legos when they go back home — his PRIZED possession. My five-year-old still misses a boy from a two-week respite. They were buddies and he fit so well into forming a little a friendly threesome with both my sons.

Our nine-month-old foster daughter has now been with us since she was three days old. The boys fell in love instantly. They treat her like a princess and are constantly fighting to see who can make her smile and laugh. I find joy when I go to my son's class and the kids ask how our daughter from foster care is doing. Our boys are educating their friends about it; spreading curiosity and hope. And it amazes me when some of these children's parents reach out about foster care wanting to know more because of OUR KIDS!!

We have seen the boys get excited when someone new is expected, and disappointed if they end up not coming. Overall, the boys feel "the more the merrier" with their foster siblings and haven't felt that it's detracted from the love and care they get from us. They have shown a great capacity for love, maturity in listening to other kid's heartaches, and are champions for what we do. We couldn't do this without their great attitudes and support.

—Laura

There have been some who told me of their concern that being a foster parent might in some way influence their own children in a negative fashion. They voiced concern that the children from foster care bring a negative influence to their own children. Instead, I think it is the opposite. My own children have been influenced in such positive ways from those they have lived with, have played alongside, have learned from, and have come to love. Our children have been introduced to a diversity of cultural beliefs and ways of thinking and have come to embrace some of these differences, as well. Additionally, my children have learned the joys that are found in adoption, — from the three that we have adopted from foster care — and have learned that families come in different shapes, colors, and sizes. My own family, as a foster family, has included children from so many different ethnic identities and cultures. As a result, my own children have so much more insight into how others live and think than most their age. In short, when you care for children in foster care in your home and your family, you will be given the opportunity to show your children how to be giving, how to be considerate of others, how to share belongings and time, and how to be sensitive and understanding to the pain that others might be suffering from, and you can do so in a very real, very hands on, very relevant fashion.

One thing I can assure you is this: your own children will be more responsible and more mature than other children their age while you are a foster family. In fact, studies have found this to be the case. A study by Twigg, from the Social Work University of Regina, Canada noted that younger biological children matured at an earlier rate to interact with their older foster siblings. The same study indicated that older biological children also matured earlier so that they could help take care of their younger foster siblings. I have seen this time and time again in my own home, as I have watched, with pleasure and pride, my children help clothe, feed, and simply care for the younger foster siblings in their home, and how they truly enjoyed doing so, in loving fashion. Another study, this time by author and researcher Angie Watson, found that biological children were "expected to be more understanding, and not retaliate, to put someone else's needs before their own." Author and researcher Wendy Spears noted that "generally those who were older thought fostering was easier because they led separate lives from the foster children and their presence did not impinge on them." The same can be said about my own older children. While they enjoy being an older foster sibling, and certainly do help out, their lives as teenagers have not been changed in a negative fashion, as they have their own lives, so to speak. I believe that my own children even take pride in being identified as a foster family and have embraced that part of their identity has been defined by their experiences as a foster sibling. Let's look at what one foster sibling had to tell me.

KOLBY'S STORY

I have been a foster sister for 14 years. I have seen over 50 children go in and out of my house, ages ranging from straight out of the hospital as a newborn up to 17 years of age. There were a lot of difficult times, but the happy times made it all worth it. Sometimes we would have children that were my age, so I went to school with them; it was awkward for me and for them. Most of the children had been through traumatizing experiences before they were put into foster care so that made it hard to communicate with them because they were often shy and scared, and tended to keep to themselves. As well as shy, some of the children were very angry and would lash out at the slightest instance. This made it difficult for me to talk to them and try to be their friend/sister when they were being loud or non-responsive. Though these were troubling times for all of us, this behavior normally happened in the first few weeks of their arrival. Once they warmed up to us and we warmed up to them, it was easier to communicate with them and genuinely enjoy their company. With some of the children that stayed for more than few months, I began to get attached to not only the cute little ones, but to the teenagers too. With those who stayed with us for a long time, we have tried our best to keep in touch and check up on them and even visit with them every so often.

Every time there was a foster child in need of a home, our home, my parents would gather everybody around the dinner table and talk to us about what we thought about inviting someone else into our home. I really respected the fact that they honored our thoughts and how we felt about the decision. Even though I knew it would be hard at times to have so many children in our home, I always tried to think of the children and how their needs should be put before mine, because I took my happy, wonderful life for granted. Seeing those children and what they went through is horrific and bringing them into our home truly enriched my life and theirs. Being a foster sister has made me a better person and has made me want to help others like my parents have. Even through the rough times, I have truly enjoyed my experience over the past 14 years, and I feel blessed to have been able to comfort and be with all those children.

—Kolby

When you decide to become a foster family, you not only need to prepare yourself, but prepare your children, as well. After all, their lives are going to change too. Your children will not only be sharing their home, but they will be sharing you, their parents. This can be difficult for them to understand, and they will need your support more than ever. To be sure, there will be questions from them and they may feel concerned, worried, and confused. In our own home, my wife and I try to include our own children in the decision-making process when it comes to having a new child placed in our family. We do this by giving some information about the child and ask them how they feel about it. It is important for you and your family that your children feel comfortable with the decision. It is just as important for you to consider your own children's feeling and concerns before you have a child from foster care placed in your home.

On one occasion, we had to decline having a particular child placed in our home because we felt our own son would be placed at risk. You see, the child from foster care was a 14-year-old teenage girl who had already had been pregnant twice and had had two abortions. My wife and I both felt that not only would it be uncomfortable for our teenage son, as he knew her from school, but that it also placed him in danger if she should make a false accusation of some kind or another against him, or even against me.

Yes, your children will likely have questions. They will likely have questions every time a child is placed into your home, as new people join their family, and even new possible playmates. Listen, I have done this for well over a decade, and my own children have the same types of questions, every single time. It's normal curiosity on their part, and I even have the same kinds of questions, as well. Let's look at what foster mother Krystal recently wrote me.

KRYSTAL'S STORY

We have had some equally amazing and hard moments with our own children while fostering. We firmly believe they are learning a level of selflessness and compassion other parents can only hope that their children learn. You can tell your kids about the world around them, you can tell them about need, and what it means to be selfless, but it's a whole other thing to actually live it.

It has also been hard when our children see new and difficult behaviors, and the way we must parent differently. It's been hard to give up some things to be a foster family. We keep reminding our kids that sacrifice is hard, and it's okay to feel all the feelings. Even in the hard stuff I know our kids are learning a level of care and compassion that is necessary in the world.

My oldest is nine; he is extremely sentimental and holds tight to tradition and emotion. This Christmas we have a three-year-old with us, so we decided to not put all of the ornaments on the tree; we didn't want them to get knocked off and broken, so we each picked one to put up high. My son got really upset; lots of tears were shed and he honestly admitted his feelings of frustration regarding his foster sister.

My husband explained that it wasn't her fault she was with us, just as it wasn't her fault we couldn't put up the ornaments, and that we weren't doing foster care because it was easy, but because it was right. It requires sacrifice and it is hard and that's okay.

He was able to understand this, and move past those feelings and into feelings of care and love.

—Krystal

Take some time to sit down with your children and remind them why you chose to be a foster parent. If possible, give them a little training session of your own. Explain what it means to be a foster home and a foster family. More importantly, explain what it will mean to be a foster sibling. Remember, this is a time of excitement, nervousness, and perhaps even anxiety for your own children. Share with them the information they need to know about your new foster child when he comes to your home. If they are too young to understand why a child might be in foster care, then there is no reason to confuse them even more by burdening them with this information. Your little ones just don't need more information or details. Now, your older children may be curious as to why the foster child is coming to live with them. It's normal, and it's okay. You probably want to know the same thing, as well. Go ahead and share with them what you know and remind them that the foster child is probably hurting, frightened, and may reject your family in the first few days and weeks. Tell your children that it will take time to form a relationship with the foster child, their foster sibling.

SANDY'S STORY

Sometimes the hardest part is when you have to handle the kiddos from foster care differently. For example, if I take pictures I have to be sure that the kiddos aren't in the pictures. If they are, they can't be shared with anyone. Often I have to ask a child to step out of our pictures. They don't understand.

We recently went through this when we took pictures for a church directory. Sometimes a foster child acts out and you have to deal with the teacher or school staff. I can't share what happened to cause this child to act a certain way because it violates privacy policy. However, that's not a problem with a biological child. I have heard my bio children say numerous times, "You let the fosters get away with everything." We can't discipline them the same way as our own and even simple things like restriction and taking items away from a foster can violate our child welfare agency's policy. Plus, you have to live in fear that if you discipline this child and it upsets the child, then you have to deal with the case worker and birth family. All of this means that we have to handle them with caution, and the fosters learn quickly that they can and often do get away with more.

These children often require more of our time and attention (therapy, visitations, etc.) and often child welfare doesn't realize just how often our bios get put on the backburner to meet the kiddos and child welfare's needs and deadlines, which often leads to resentment from our bio children. As far as blessings, children come into our home and we do our very best to make them feel as welcome as possible. Most kids come in scared, but quickly open up and find their special place in our family and hearts. However, recently I asked one of my older children why they don't really acknowledge the baby in our home and she said because she knows she is going to leave and she doesn't want to get attached because it hurts so badly. The sad part is that this child has been with us two-and-a-half years, but because this case is so complicated my child is just too scared.

—Sandy

As I wrote earlier, your own children may have concerns. Perhaps they are worried that they will have to share you with their new foster sibling. They may resent that there is a new person joining their family, sharing their toys, and sharing their parents. They may have feelings of jealousy or even feelings of anger. They might even be scared or worried. My own children have had some of these feelings, and yours most likely will have one or all of these at some point. It's normal. Indeed, every child from a foster parent family will experience one of these at some point. Even more so, there may be feelings of guilt from a biological child, stemming from the fact that they are struggling with their feelings and emotions and don't want to up- set their parents. Again, these are all common feelings. As a parent, you will need to reassure your child that their feelings and concerns are OK, and that they are heard and understood by you. They need this validation. Ask them to share their feelings with you and listen to what they have to say. Reassure your own children that you will always be there for them.

Perhaps one of the biggest concerns your own child has is if they will lose you as a parent to the new sibling and foster child in your home. Without a doubt, it can be a very time-consuming job on your behalf, as you care for children who are demanding of both your time and emotions. We have seen throughout this book that foster parenting is full-time work. Thus, it is vital that you do not let your own children slip through the cracks; en- sure that they receive the necessary time, love, and affection from you. You will want to set aside some special time for just you and your own children, as they will need time alone with you during your fostering. You can do this, of course, in a number of ways. Spend some one-on-one time alone with your child. Take him fishing, go see a movie with her, teach him how to fly a kite, bake cookies and get the kitchen messy with her, play basket- ball with him, go for a bike ride with her, take him to get ice cream, go out to dinner with her. There are so many things you can do with your own child that includes just the two of you. If you have more than one child, like I do, try to set aside some time with each one individually. To be sure, that can be difficult, but it is so very important.

What Your Children Need To Hear

During my 20 years as a parent, I have had the pleasure of being a parent to over 50 children. Yes, 50 plus children, including biological, adoptive, foster care, and homeless youth. These children came from all walks of life, backgrounds, cultures, and appearances before living with me and becoming a part of my family. During this time, I discovered that there are some things, some words that every child needs to hear from their parents, whether they are your own biological children or children from foster care living with you as part of your family.

Words **do** have power. Words can heal, and they can hurt. Words can encourage, and they can destroy. The power we have when we speak is indeed significant, and can be life-changing and mountain-moving. Words of affirmation, trust, and compassion are building blocks in the life of a child. Words of patience, kindness, and love are essential to the well-being, mental health, and emotional stability of each child. As a parent, I understand that what I say to my children is influential to their development. Now, there are five things every child needs to hear from their parents. Let's look at these.

1. "I love you"

Sadly, I have found over the years as a foster parent that so many children have never heard these three important words. Yet, these three words are the most important words that they need to hear. Indeed, one can never say, "I love you," to a child enough times. They need to and deserve to hear it several times a day. "I love you," reminds children that they are valuable, that they matter, and that someone truly cares for them. How often are you telling your own children this? I hope it is at least once a day. If they aren't hearing it from you, they will seek it from someone else.

2. "I'm proud of you"

Children need a cheerleader. They need to know that someone believes in them. They need to know that what they do matters. When you tell a child that you are proud of him, it only encourages him to work even harder. Celebrate each little success a child has, no matter how small it might be.

3. "I'm sorry"

I am in no way a perfect parent. Despite parenting over 50 children, I am no expert and have made countless mistakes. I will continue to make mistakes, because, quite frankly, I am human. When I make a mistake and disappoint or hurt a child in some way, it is important for me to say that "I'm sorry." Pride should never get in the way of this. You should never be too proud to ask a child for forgiveness. Not only are we letting children know that we have accepted our own poor choices and mistakes, we are teaching children that it is important to take ownership of their own mistakes.

4. "I forgive you"

Children are bound to make mistakes, just like you and I are. Forgiveness is a powerful gift that we can give each other, one we certainly need to give to our children. Love and forgiveness are two actions that are intertwined and cannot be separated. If we truly love others, then we need to forgive, as well. Without forgiveness, there is no love. When a child makes a mistake or a poor choice, they need to hear that they are forgiven. They need to hear from their parents that no matter what, you forgive them, and you love them.

5. "I am thankful for you"

As a parent, I understand that what I say to my children is instrumental to their development. Each day, I try to find something positive to say to each child and thank them for something they did throughout the day. Whether it is praising a child for unloading the dishwasher or how their hair looked, I understand that my children crave a kind word from me. As a former high school teacher, I tried to find some way to compliment each student on a regular basis, never speaking harshly or negatively, and showing kindness in my deeds and my words. In both worlds, as a parent and as a teacher, the words "please" and "thank you" were a large part of my vocabulary, and I tried to not only use them throughout each day, but model them as examples for their own way of speech. I do the same with each child that lives in my home. "Thank you" reminds the child that what they are doing is recognized, is appreciated, and does matter. Like "I love you," a parent needs to find something to thank their child for each day.

CHAPTER 8

Working With Your Foster Child's Family

I must be honest with you. My wife is much better at working with the birth parents of my children in foster care. You see, there are times when I am not as welcoming as she is. There are times when I am a little frustrated with the birth parents, due to the abuse and neglect they may have inflicted upon my foster care children whom I consider a part of my family. When a child from foster care is placed into my home, that child becomes a child of my own; a child that I love unconditionally and will fight for with all my strength and resources to protect him from further harm and trauma. With this in mind, I sometimes have a difficult time getting past my own judgmental nature, and that is so very wrong of me. I know this, and I work hard at getting past this weakness of mine.

As I noted above, my wife is much better at this and is a very loving and caring person; it is one of her strengths. I understand the importance of creating a healthy and positive working relationship with the birth parents of my foster children. After all, the end goal is that of reunification between the child and the parent. As foster parents, we want to ensure that we do the best we can with the birth parents so that the child living with us, the child that has become a part of our own family, has a happy, healthy, and safe home to go back to.

KRISTIN'S STORY

My biggest frustration with fostering is when the bio parents try to pick apart my parenting and find fault with every small detail. Social workers sometimes feed this blame frenzy. I am certainly aware this is their transference from their own insecurities and have learned how to be proactive in making things work with all sorts of families. I have had parents that looked at a child that had a virus with sores in his mouth (hand, foot, and mouth) and they made the accusation I let this child drink boiling-hot liquid or allowed him to chew on a battery. I immediately took this child to urgent care to have it recorded and documented that this was from a virus to prevent any problems and stay one step ahead of any accusations. I have learned to take these things in stride and be pro-active to protect these kids, my family, and myself.

I have also had parents that did not want baby powder, bibs, or other common items used on their babies/children and have learned to accommodate these as much as possible to create as much of a co-parenting environment as possible and give them some feeling of control in their kids' lives outside of their home.

I have had parents make accusations about everything from feeding kids incorrectly to not getting their prescription filled. I have made sure to have every change (formula or diet) documented by health professionals and keep accurate records of any necessary health changes to keep everything as clear as possible. I see the foster parents as being in the "Hot Seat," so to speak, as all other parties are watching closely and scrutinizing actions which can be a great, difficult, and rewarding challenge.

—Kristin

To be sure, it can be difficult having a foster child in your home. He may have been placed in your home because of abuse or neglect from his family. Perhaps he was in danger from parents who were abusing themselves. Whatever the reason for his placement into Child Welfare's custody, your foster child has most likely come with some emotional problems and is struggling with the loss of his family. As a foster parent, it is part of your job to help your foster child deal with these issues and help him adjust to his new environment, as well as develop a positive and loving relationship with him.

With that in mind, what can be more difficult is another part of your role as a foster parent: working with birth parents. It can be difficult, and it can be stressful at times. Indeed, there are times when it just might not be possible. What is best for your foster child, though, is that you work alongside your caseworker, as well as the birth parents, and try to determine what is best for your foster child's future, as well as how to best meet his needs in the present.

As foster parents, part of our job, so to speak, is co-parenting. When a foster parent shares the role of nurturing a foster child with the birth parents and caseworker, reunification tends to happen at a quicker and more successful rate. Co-parenting means that you, as a foster parent, work alongside the biological parents of the child living under your roof, and with your family. This may be the more difficult part of your job. To begin with, these may be the people who abused or neglected your foster child. Helping them might just be the last thing you wish to do. Indeed, your first inclination may be that these are people who do not deserve to have their child back or have any say in how you raise them. That's human nature, my friend. That's normal. You became a foster parent because you have a heart for children, you care about kids in need, you want to help them and protect them, and you want to give them a home where they are loved.

At the same time, we are also here to help the parents of the children that we are caring for. Therefore, it is important that you do not prejudge the birth parents and biological family members before you meet them. What is important to consider, though, is that many biological parents of foster children were abused themselves and know of no other way of raising children. Also disturbing is that some birth parents were foster children as well, and they are just repeating the cycle they went through as a child. This is the case for two of my own children who are third-generation foster care. Third generation — let that sink in. That means that the parents *and* grandparents of two of the children I have adopted from foster care were also in the system. Certainly, there are reasons why their children are in care that we may never understand. What is best for your foster child, though, is that you work alongside your caseworker, as well as the birth parents, and try to determine what is best for your foster child's future, as well as how to best meet his needs in the present.

There are those biological parents who will be happy to work with you. They will not only be eager to work alongside you in order to be reunited with their child, but may also wish to learn how to better their parenting skills from you. They will appreciate that you are taking care of their child and will be grateful for all that you do for him. You might be providing more opportunities for him than they were ever able to do themselves, such as clothing, medical care, and material items. They may be grateful that he is in a house that has enough food for him, as well as appreciate that he is in a clean and safe home. These birth parents may even be thankful that he is in an environment where their child is getting a better education.

At the same time, there are also those families that are angry with the child welfare agency, and feel that their child was taken away unnecessarily. What's more, there are those birth parents that are resentful to you for having their child placed in your home. My friend, they may see you as the enemy and find fault with all you do. These biological parents may even verbally assault you in a meeting with the caseworker or in front of their own children. Let's look at what one foster parents recently told me.

CHAR'S STORY

We have a birth mother who is constantly telling her girls not to call us 'Mom' and 'Dad' because they are her mom and dad, not us. We tell all of our children that they can call us by our first names or Mom and Dad, whichever they're more comfortable with. We tell them and the parents that the kids now have two sets of parents, all of whom love them. This particular set of parents doesn't seem to like that answer.

—Char

Like Char, this has happened to me on occasion, as well, and I have learned not to take it personally, as I recognize that it simply may be that person is suffering from pain, and unresolved trauma or anxiety in their own life. Sadly, this type of situation turns some foster parents off from fostering more children, and drives them away from the system. Again, it is important to keep in mind that these biological parents are hurting in their own way and are struggling with their own personal issues. Lashing out towards you may be the only way they know to release their frustrations.

Many child welfare agencies have begun to recently ask for foster parents to become more involved with birth parents. Caseworkers are asking foster parents to reach out to birth parents through phone calls, emails, and face-to-face meetings. Child welfare agencies are encouraging both foster parents and birth families to work alongside each other in the hope of reuniting child and family together. Not only will the foster child benefit from this cooperative relationship, but it is hoped that the biological parents may also benefit, as they learn positive parenting skills from the foster parents. There are a number of stress-reducing strategies that you, as a foster parent, can use when working with birth parents.

Being a Role Model to the Birth Family

You are a role model.

So am I. So is each one of us. Unfortunately, there aren't many good ones these days. There are far too many poor role models for our kids to watch and mimic. You and I need to step it up and help change that. We need to take our role of being a good parent more seriously. We need to embrace the possibility that we might be the only positive role model other children might ever see.

There will always be someone who is watching us, listening to us, and perhaps even modeling after us. Somebody is watching what you do today. Someone is listening to what you say. Maybe it is your child. Perhaps it is a niece, nephew, or grandchild. It might be the child at the grocery store, watching you stroll down the aisle or pack up your items at the check-out line. As a role model, what kind of message are you sending? What kind of lesson are you teaching to the younger generation?

As foster parents, we need to not only understand this role, but embrace it. We are role models not only for the children living in our homes and as our family members, but also for the birth parents and our own biological children.

People like 22-year-old mother Mireya Alejandra Lopez, who drowned two of her twin infants in a bathtub, lack love in their life. When questioned by investigators, Mireya stated that nobody loved her children and nobody loved her. People like Dylann Roof, the alleged shooter of nine people in Charleston, South Carolina, had few good role models in their lives or homes. With an absent mother and a father who beat his step-mother, by age 15, Dylann began skipping classes, eventually quit school, and ended up unemployed and taking drugs. 15-year old Alyssa Bustamante, who brutally stabbed a nine-year-old girl, simply because she "wanted to know what it was like to kill people," also suffered from lack of healthy parenting. Abandoned by her mother and a father who was in prison for most of her childhood, the troubled teen battled depression and thoughts of suicide.

As a parent, you will be a role model for countless people, and many eyes will be upon you. Not only will you be a role model for your children, but for the public as a whole. For your neighbor who is having a difficult time as a parent, you are a role model. For the inexperieced expecting mother at work, you are a role model. For your child's friend who comes from a home of abuse, you are a role model. After all, not many in our society know what good parenting is really about these days. Your actions today might show other parents and other children how to act, how to behave, how to be compassionate, and how to be kind. People are watching you, today. People are learning from you, today. I am an adoptive and foster parent, and have been, for 13 years now, taking care of 45 plus children in my home and in my family. My family, my work mates, close friends, those at my church, all will discover what foster care is all about and what good parenting is about, just by watching what I do each and every day. If you are a foster parent, everything you do will send signals to the biological parents about how a parent should act, as well as how to treat their own children. Everything you say will speak volumes to the child's birth family members.

JESSICA'S STORY

The woman who led our parent training said these words to us: "But by the grace of God, there go I." She was referring to the parents of our little ones. It's so easy to pass judgment on mothers and fathers who have their children taken away from them. It can be so easy to write them off as "garbage," "crap," or even worse terms. These are things I have had people actually say to me in regards to biological parents of foster children. Unfortunately, we are creatures of experience, and this broken system we live in is cyclical. We easily repeat cycles of what we have lived and it's only by the grace of God that I grew up the way that I did, where I did, with the people I did. These parents deserve love and someone to believe in them as much as their kids because chances are, they were once in those same shoes.

Last week I met the mother of my child.

I went to my first court date about 10 days ago for our little girl. I was not sure what to expect but knew that, according to my training, it's beneficial to all stakeholders if the bio and foster parents work together and form some sort of relationship. My caseworker asked if I wanted to meet Mia's mom, and I nervously agreed. Would she like me? Was she going to be hateful? Would I unintentionally come off as "judgy?" What do I say? But before I could process my thoughts, I saw her. There she was — no older than myself, standing with her boyfriend right in front of me. What came out of my mouth was something like, "Hello, my name is Jessica and Mia is staying with me and my husband for now."

To my complete surprise, she shook my hand and was happy to meet me! Not even 60 seconds had gone by before I was showing her videos and pictures of her little girl, and we were exchanging stories about Mia. She was able to fill me on some much needed medical information, and I let her brag about how awesome her baby girl is for almost a full hour before we were called for our turn in court. It was so cool how God was able to connect us to one another, and the mutual love we shared for Mia was evident. This lady was not the scum of the earth. This was my girl's mother! What's even better is that she was not hoping for my failure as a parent. Rather, she was giving me insight on what her daughter likes and sharing stories so I could know her background more. She wanted me to succeed in loving her little girl! What an honor!

I would be lying if I denied that I had moments of jealousy, jealousy that I couldn't call her daughter my own permanently, and sadness that I would have to say goodbye someday. Pangs of emotion ran through me, and I immediately wanted to go pick Mia up from daycare to hold her tight because one day she wouldn't be there. But for now, I focus on the total win that God gave to me in that court hall when a mother, who could have been envious and hateful towards me, responded with humility and support for the sake of her baby. My daughter's family is not perfect, but they are her family. I have been able to pray for them better since meeting her mother because this is no longer a case file I have only read through. God has entrusted us with a responsibility to pray and intercede on the behalf of not just our child, but her family as well!

—Jessica

Time for Questions

I have always had questions about everything. I just want to know about things. My wife gets a little sick of my questions from time to time. I imagine that some of the caseworkers I have worked with have, as well. I am just a curious kind of guy. You probably are, too, when it comes to the children living in your home and with your family.

I have found that the more information I have about my foster children, the better prepared I am to help them. Indeed, knowledge is power, as we both know. Often, the best place to find those answers is from the parents and family members of the foster child living in your home. After all, it is likely that your foster child's biological parents and family members will know him better than anyone, even the case worker. You might just have an opportunity to find out some of the answers you are seeking about your foster child, as well as discover more about him from his family. Face-to-face meetings and phone conversations with the birth parents and biological family members can help both you and the child. Your meetings with them will offer you the opportunity to learn a great deal about the foster child in your home, including his likes and dislikes, his hobbies and interests, his fears and concerns, what foods he enjoys, and much more.

Along with this, you can also acquire important information you might need. This information might include how he performs in school, struggles he faces in the classroom, allergies, medical history and concerns, and more. Along with this, when you ask questions about their child, you are showing the birth parents that you are interested in him and his well-being. This will only help you and the child, as well as comfort and reassure the parents that you are on the side of their child, and that you are looking out for his best interests. By indicating, with your questions, that his parents are the experts, you will begin to form an important relationship, one that will benefit all involved. Again, make sure you ask these questions with respect, kindness, and understanding. In no way do you want the upset or offend the birth parents, or show them any sign of disrespect. This will only hurt the child in both the short-term and long-term.

You need to come prepared to a meeting with the birth parents. What better way to come prepared than to have a list of questions with you? I would encourage you to let the child's caseworker know beforchand that you would like to ask his birth parents or biological family members some questions. A list of questions prepared beforehand will help you gather the information you need. You might have these questions written down on paper in a folder or notebook. These questions may include the child's likes and dislikes, favorite toys and games, health and medical history, school background and educational needs, his strengths and weaknesses, behavior concerns, regular home routines, and other information that will help you better understand the child. Remember, when you ask these questions, you are showing interest in the child and allowing the parents to be the expert on their child. It also shows that you respect their opinion. This will go a long way towards not only building a positive and healthy working relationship with the child's parents, but also in allowing the parent to begin to heal in their own way, as well.

Just like you have questions, so will others. This time, the questions might be pointed towards you, about you, or be centered on your family. Your foster child's biological family will no doubt be very curious about you. Once again, that is normal and healthy. After all, you are caring for their child. The biological family and birth parents want to know all about you: what you do, who you are, why you are a foster parent, if you are doing a good job, and perhaps most importantly, if the child is safe and cared for in your home. If you think about it, you would most likely have these same questions if the roles were reversed, and your own child was living in another home with another family.

Now, the birth parents you work with may be uncomfortable or might not feel that they can ask questions of you and your family. If that's the case, feel free to share with them some information about you and the family their child is living with. Show them that your family is excited and happy to have their child come stay with you during this time. Reassure them that their child will be safe with you and that you will provide an environment and home where their child will be safe and cared for. The more you reassure the birth parents that their child will be cared for and looked after, the better your relationship will be with them.

Visitations

STEPHANIE'S STORY

One of our biggest challenges has been seeing the birth mother of our daughter show up high to a visit. She was so high she almost dropped our infant daughter! We had to walk away and let the visit happen because it was court-ordered and the social worker was to monitor the visit. At the end of the visit, the birth mom was coming down from her drug of choice and was being a royal pain! We tried to quickly gather our daughter and her brothers; please note the term "tried!" The birth parents caused a scene because the older siblings ran from them to my husband and me. Then, to end a delightful evening, the birth mom decided that she was taking the folders she had bought for one of the older siblings because she did not like his attitude! Cue meltdown! We got all the kids outside, sent the birth parents one way, and then had to reason with a five-year-old about choices and who was in charges of his choices. Meanwhile, the social worker was trying to regain control of entire situation.

—Stephanie

Too many times, I would walk into the child welfare agency's visitation room, and find a child I am caring for staring out the window, waiting for her mother to visit, with tears streaming down her face. Each time, my own heart is filled with sadness for this little child who was torn away from the only family she knew and placed with us, strangers in a strange home. "Why didn't my mommy come?" the child might ask me, between sobs.

"Sweetheart, maybe she's sick," I might answer one week. Another week, when faced with the same question, I would answer her with "Maybe her car is not working." How could I explain to a seven-year-old girl that her mother failed a drug test or simply couldn't be bothered to show up? It isn't fair to the child, and there are times when I feel anger towards the parent. I know it's wrong of me to be judgmental, so I try not to have these feelings.

Unfortunately, there are times when schedules do not go as planned and individuals are let down. For children in foster care, this can be especially difficult when it comes to visitations with birth parents and biological family members. As one who has watched many of my own foster children come home from disappointing visitations, my own heart has broken as these children struggle to figure out why their mother or father did not come to see them.

For children in foster care, visitations with family members are often an event that they look forward to with great eagerness. After all, they are seeing their parents or other family members, and being reunited with them, if only for a very brief time. Often times, visitations are held at child welfare agencies, while other times they are held in neutral locations, such as restaurants, parks, and even faith-based institutions. The time usually flies by quickly, and the child and biological family member are once again separated until the next meeting. Visitations are important for a number of reasons and help maintain the relationship between both child and adult.

Yet, there are times when a biological family member cannot make it, for whatever reason, and the scheduled visit is cancelled. Too many times, these children are left wondering why their parents did not show. Self-doubt sets in, as they question if it was something they may have done, or perhaps if their parents were mad at them. Some may believe that their parents don't care about them, and that they do not even matter. For all involved, it is another rejection, another painful experience, and another heartbreak.

When your foster child meets his birth parents for visitations and meetings, he should be well-dressed, clean, healthy, and look his best. His hair should be combed, nails cut, clothes clean and fitting nicely. After all, you are sending a message that he is worthy of your utmost attention and care. Also important is the time factor. Quite simply, be on time. Perhaps you know the old adage that I learned a long time ago. It goes like this, "When you are early, you are on time. When you are on time, you are late. And when you are late, it is a sin." Well, we need to follow that, as well. Be early to your child's visitation, if possible, so you can be on time. When you are late to a visitation, it may send the mistaken message to the birth parents that you do not value their time or that you don't take the visitation seriously, and that you might not be bothered to make the effort. Along with that, do not cut the visitation short for your own appointments, either.

You can also help the birth parents, as well as the child and yourself, by preparing beforehand when visitations and meetings are scheduled. Don't be afraid to feed the child beforehand, whether the visitation takes place around lunchtime, or around dinner. This will not only relieve some of the pressure off of the birth parents to provide food to the child, it may also help you when the child returns home. Along with this, it allows you control of the child's diet and food intake. Far too many times, children have returned to my own home, sugared up, so to speak, with junk food. As we are a family that has a healthy diet and meals as part of our everyday life, junk food can have negative effects, in a number of ways, on the child afterwards.

SARAH'S STORY

When George was 14, he came to visit his older brother who was living in our home. After several weekend visits, the boys approached us about George moving from the foster home he was currently in to our home because they had been apart for almost two years. After much talk as a family, we decided to move forward with this idea and spoke with his case manager. In a matter of days, several conversations and a waiver to accept one more child, we were a family of 8!

To say this child became special quickly is an understatement. Over the course of a year, I watched him grow into a young man. He flourished at school, joined sports teams and clubs, made friends. I watched his grades improve, his attitude change, and he even began to call us Mom and Dad. When asked by his case manager, he told her he wanted to continue to live with us and felt no desire to go back to his bio mom. He had good, well thought-out reasons, and, for a time, his siblings were on board.

On the appointed court date, the plan was to ask for non-reunification, but for visits to continue. The case that the child welfare office had was strong, but one of the siblings changed their mind and talked the others into following suit. Even after hearing George's concerns, the judge decided to send the girl home, the older boy was 18 and decided to stay in foster care until he finished high school, and we were to spend the three summer months transitioning George to his bio mom.

Over the summer, he would make contact with his bio mom and have an overnight visit every other week. He came home with stories of strangers being there all hours of the night, fights, and partying. We knew he was uncomfortable. Just before the three-month mark, his sister was taken back into child welfare custody, and shortly after, she also became a very special part of our family.

On October 24, we had another court date. We were assured there was no way they were going back, and they were prepared to begin Termination of Parental Rights, or TPR. There was no hearing. George's Guardian ad Litem (the volunteer appointed by the court help the child), the Department's attorney, and the mother's attorney came to an agreement to send them back to their bio mom, and the judge agreed. No evidence was given, no testimony heard, no consideration to the fact that these children have been in care more than three times in their lives, this time for more than three years. We were directed to bring them back to our house, get their stuff and deliver them to their bio mom's house. And that we did.

A month later, I still speak to them every day on the phone, but they are not allowed to visit us, or the four boys who have become their brothers. Every morning, I tell them I love them, and again every night before bed. Sometimes I do it a dozen times in between. We were not prepared to lose them. My heart aches. I miss the late night conversations over hot chocolate, sitting at the island doing homework at the same time while listening to his ridiculous music, and hollering for him to turn his clothes right side out. I miss the stinky hugs after football practice, the huge grocery bill, and the house full of football players all weekend.

Now, I look for him at school every day, and most days, he's not there. They've been to school fewer days than they've missed, they're failing all of their classes, among many other things that are going wrong. I pray a million times a day that one of them is going to wake up and realize that they have to be in control of the way their life turns out. Until then, we just offer them our love and support from afar. Until the day he turns 18, we will always leave a spot open, just in case he needs to come home.

—Sarah

Being There

It might not always be easy. It might not always be pleasant. Yet, your role as a foster parent is to not only to help the children in need, but work towards reunification of the child with his family. Does this always happen? No. Should it always happen? Well, I have seen occasions where the child was placed in harm's way when returned to his family and his home when he was better off with his foster family, which is a tragedy on many levels. On the other hand, I have seen children return to their families and have the "happy ending" we all hoped for and worked towards. I have seen families reunite, thrive, and succeed.

As foster parents, we have the opportunity to help bring families together, to help children heal, and to help biological family members be better parents and caretakers. Through our actions and words, through our questions and answers, and through our compassion and patience, we can help in the healing process for all involved. As a foster parent, you are a role model not only for the child, but also for his parents, your friends and family, and for society. As a foster parent, you have the ability to give words of comfort and love to both the child and his family. As a foster parent, you can teach life lessons and help both child and parent learn new skills. What a great opportunity — and big responsibility. I know you are up to the task! I know you will do a great job!

CHAPTER 9

Finding the Help You Need

When I speak to my fellow foster parents across the nation, I remind them that no one truly understands a foster parent like another foster parent. We live a life that is so different from others, and a lifestyle that few totally appreciate or understand. Even my own family doesn't understand what my wife and I truly do, and I have written several books on the subject.

Just the other day, a journalist asked me what a typical day at my home was like. I explained to her that it is nonstop. Each day in my home, we run both the dish washer and washing machine three times, we go through two to three gallons of milk, two boxes of cereal, and at least one loaf of bread. Financially, it can be a real struggle, despite the help and assistance from the per diem, and despite what the public, and even our friends may think. Yes, I have also heard, several times, that foster parents are in it for the money. If only they knew, right? Then, there are the doctor appointments, visitations, court appointments, sporting events, and everything else involved. There is truly very little time to relax. You and I both know that it is exhausting.

As we have seen throughout this book, foster parents can easily become worn down, burned out, exhausted, and frustrated. They feel grief and loss, and become overwhelmed. The struggle is real, my friend. Perhaps this is why so many people either choose not to become a foster parent or quit fostering after 18 months, the average length of time most individuals remain foster parents.

Along with this is the struggle to stay positive in the face of anxiety, trauma, angry bio parents, care for children who are suffering, and a court system that doesn't seem to understand. Then, of course, is, our daily work schedule, bills that seem to pile up on the kitchen counter, the needs of our own family members and even ourselves. Add on top of that the negative stigma and beliefs about foster care and foster parenting that are in the media and news each day, as well as the strange looks and whispers from others about us, simply because we are foster parents. Yes, sometimes it is hard to remain positive, especially in front of the children who need us to do so, each day and each moment.

TAMMY'S STORY

I am a single mom. I am raising two grandkids that are 13 and 14 years old. I foster children that have been from three years old to 12 years old. I have been through loss and grief twice. I miss all the kids and always cry once they leave, but there were two children at different times that I was going to adopt. One went back to her bio mom, and was then taken and put in another home that adopted her. The second was an open-and-shut case in which, all of a sudden, her grandmother came out of nowhere and I lost her. I cried so hard and was wondering if I should stop fostering.

I thought I was just burned out, but I looked at the photos of 25 children that I have had and just couldn't. Self-care is out of the question. I haven't taken time for myself in three years. I am not sure what happened, I just noticed one day I was falling apart at the seams. I wasn't wearing makeup or spending time doing things I like to do. I used to paint ceramics. I have since packed them all away. I don't even color in the adult coloring books.

My home has suffered, the carpet is ruined and needs replaced, I have had some holes in my walls, and almost all the window screens are broken and need to be replaced. There is so much to do in my home, but I don't have enough time in the day with the kids as it is. But I wouldn't give this up for anything. These children need a home where they feel safe and loved. So I keep going.

—Tammy

A Support Group of People Just Like You

You probably have a support group of some kind, people that you surround yourself with in order to find encouragement and strength; people who help you in times of need and lift you up when you are struggling; people who understand you and make you laugh and feel better, even in the most difficult of times; people you can count on to be there for you. Your support group might be members of your family, your friends, people at work, or perhaps fellow church members.

As a foster parent, you will need a support group. To be sure, your friends and family members can, and hopefully will, offer you support as a foster parent and be there to help out in times of struggle. Yet, you will find that you will need another group of people to surround yourself with. For you see, your own friends and family members may at some point question whether or not you should continue to be a foster parent, whether out of concern for your well-being, confusion about what you are doing, or maybe even possibly from their own guilt that they are not doing enough themselves. These questions from your friends and family members are normal. I have heard them time and time again from my own dear friends and family.

You might also have found, or will soon find, that you are not invited to all the parties, gatherings, and events that you once used to be invited to. You may find that your friends are now doing things with others, and that there is a distance growing between you and other people. Some may feel that the children you are caring for are "too rowdy", and no longer want you in their homes. Soon, you may feel lonely, isolated, and feel like you have no one to talk to. As I noted earlier, no one will truly understand you and what you do like another who has walked in your shoes and lived your lifestyle as a foster parent. Let's look at what Pam experienced as a foster parent.

PAM'S STORY

We never realized that our emotions and feelings would be like a roller-coaster ride. We would go from being a happy family unit of five to a family unit that became afraid to breathe. We felt fear and were always looking over our shoulders. We did not know who we could trust, and we soon found out that your life can change in the blink of an eye. We went from having tons of friends and enjoying outings with other foster families to being totally alone. Our justice system says innocent until proven guilty; that is not the way it is in the foster care system. Once the horrible allegations started, no one was around to offer support. So much for being a team. A team sticks together until the bitter end, but not in this case. People completely shut us out, and no one offered support. All of a sudden, we went from being a great foster family to complete criminals.

People were making decisions about our lives and we were not even present during the meetings or court dates. We were completely cut out of the kids' lives. We could not see them or even ask about them. We did not have anyone that believed in us that wanted to stand with us. The only way we lived through the toughest year of our lives was our faith and belief in God. We often felt like giving up and walking away. The only reason we stayed was the kids. We were their mom and dad. We had loved them when no one else wanted them. We opened our house up to those kids and they were a part of our hearts.

So many times we asked ourselves if it was worth it and I can answer that by saying when you walk into a room and that child's face lights up. They begin running to you and you hear cries of "Mommy." That is what makes the pain, the broken heart, the tears, the fear, and the feeling of the out of control roller-coaster ride easier to withstand.

—Pam

Perhaps the best thing a caseworker ever helped me with was setting up a foster parent association, or support group, in the small town in which I lived. When my wife and I became licensed, so many years ago it seems, we did so with four other families in our rural town. At that time, there was no foster parent support group. Though I did not see the importance at that time, my caseworker did, and she helped all of us new foster parents organize a support group that met monthly. I can tell you, without hesitation, it saved my sanity on more than one occasion. I just love my foster parent support group, and truly enjoy going to each meeting.

A foster parent association or support group gives you the opportunity to find the support system you need and deserve, and to develop relationships and friendships with other foster parents, just like you. These relationships and new friendships are great opportunities for you to validate your own experiences and emotions you feel while caring for children from foster care in your home. You will also have the opportunity to share with your fellow foster parents some of the challenges, frustrations, and difficulties that you feel and experience, all without the judgment by those who don't understand you or understand the challenges that children in foster care face. You can laugh along with them at some of the craziness that comes with being a foster parent, vent your frustrations to those who understand, and cry in front of a group of people who truly appreciate what you are going through. You will find the support and encouragement that you need when you face the very unique challenges and difficulties that go along with being a foster parent.

Along with this, a strong foster parent association will provide the opportunity to learn from others, as you listen to their stories and experiences. Indeed, I have learned more from my fellow foster parents, as I listen to what they went through and how they handled it. Another great benefit from being in a foster parent support group is that you will be able to share ideas and resources with each other.

Many associations meet once a month, while others may meet every other month. It is important that you attend these meetings, as it not only keeps you connected with other foster parents and the resources they might have, but many associations include training during their meetings. We all need training, both to remain licensed and to continue to learn. Foster parent training at support group meetings can take several forms. One month, you might learn about drug and alcohol awareness, and how to best treat children who suffer from their parent's past abuse. Another month, you might get your CPR certification. Still, another month you might learn about the dangers of online technology and social media that children, especially those in foster care face; about behavior modifications; or even about how to strengthen your own marriage while caring for children in need in your home. These hours spent in training each month will go towards the yearly amount of hours you are required to have in order to remain certified as a foster parent. To be sure, as each state requires different amounts of hours of training, it will be important for you to contact your local agency and find out how many hours of training you will need each year to remain licensed.

If you are not aware of a foster parent association or support group in your area, contact your foster care agency or local child welfare agency and ask them if there is such a group that you could join in your area. If for some reason there is not a support group in your area, ask your agency if there is one nearby or get online and do a search for one near where you live. If you find one, send them a message and ask if you could join and attend meetings. The answer will probably be "yes." Of course, you can meet great foster parents at state and national foster parent conferences, and you might even see me at one of these, as well. Speaking of national foster parent conferences, there are also some fantastic national foster parent groups, as well, that you can join. Oh, and don't forget the many foster parent support groups on social media, too, many of which are listed in the resource section in the back of this book. All of these offer opportunities for you to find the support, encouragement, and wisdom you need from those just like you, your fellow foster parent.

A Support Group of Professionals

You and I both know that we can't do it all by ourselves. That's why support groups are so very important, whether it is support from our friends and family or through a foster parent association and support group. Yet, there is another type of support group that you need to surround yourself with. It is essential that you, as a foster parent, create a support group, or network if you will, of professionals specifically trained in a given occupation.

There are many early mornings when I show up at our doctor's office, with a new foster child in my arms or following through the door behind me, a child that had been placed into my home the afternoon or night before-hand. I am pretty certain that you have found, just like I have, that most children being placed into our homes are behind in their doctor appointments and vaccinations, or shots. Children are placed into our homes who are unhealthy or sick, or who might be on prescription drugs of some kind or another. Before we can enroll them into a daycare or a school system, we have to make sure that they are indeed up to date on all medical records and vaccinations, and that they are healthy. So, it is yet another trip to the doctor's office. Have you been there a lot? I sure have. It's just one more responsibility of being a foster parent. Fortunately, I have been able to form a very positive and friendly relationship with my doctor and give her some insight into all that foster care and foster parenting entail. As she has a strong heart for children, she will often find a way to see my children from foster care as soon as she possibly can, sometimes very early in the morning or late at night, if need be.

Your own professional support group should include not only doctors, but also others who can help you in a professional manner while you care for children in need in your home and family. These professionals may include child psychologists, counselors and therapists, and your child welfare worker or caseworker. Along with this, it would be wise, and helpful for you, to also include someone trained in speech pathology, a family counselor or pastor, and even an attorney that focuses on family law. Let's look at what one foster parent said about some members of her professional support group.

CAREY'S STORY

Having my own family has been a lifelong dream. Once licensed as a Foster-to-Adopt home, I took this seriously, both for myself and for the children. Soon, a four-year-old boy joined our family. He was removed from his home seven months prior due to child endangerment (opened the locked motel door he was living at and was found wandering on a highway). Placed in kinship homes up until being placed with me, I was the fourth home in less than eight months. Child Protective

Services (CPS) would do emergency removals because he would throw such horrible tantrums, was violent and destructive. He was a stress eater (only junk food) and wasn't physically able to perform most activities, much less be taken in public! The caseworker also misinformed me of Psychological Testing/appointments that were supposedly for him.

Within the first week, we were in crisis mode. This is when I first realized there was little support for me. I find it ironic that caseworkers turn their phones off after-hours or on weekends because they need a break. Friday morning, as the little one was out of control, terrorizing my little dogs and my family, I could not get a return call from my agency or CPS. I was in such distress that I called the Crisis Hotline in tears. He had serious and severe issues that would require professional help. Now I was more than frustrated and angry, I was worried.

It was a crazy road and it took a lot of phone hours to get help. I discovered the information that the previous caregiver gave me about his Psychological Evaluation never happened, and after talking to the Therapy Group and Insurance, it was determined that nothing had ever been done for this little boy. How could this happen and how could the paperwork state otherwise? I was overwhelmed at this point, losing trust and faith in a system that had NO idea what this little boy had experienced, not only before his removal but afterwards as well.

I found a place in Texas that works on CPS cases and got him in the next day for a Psychological Evaluation. Then we did Speech Evaluation, Occupational Therapy Evaluation, and Play Therapy. Our foster son has severe PTSD with multiple sensory/developmental problems and delays, probable abuse, and trauma; the list was long. During all this time, my Agency worker was not supportive because of the conflicting information in the paperwork, and continued going on the previous caregiver's word, insisting he was just a normal four-and-half-year-old.

Testing later showed what everyone assumed was ADHD was actually severe sensory and developmental issues! They were trying to communicate with a two-year old inside a four-and-a-half-year-old body with the fine motor skills of a 15-30-month-old.

I learned that you need a great agency! I recently had a new agency worker to take over my case, and she got the ball moving immediately to get me gift cards for clothing, helped get information to the accounting department of the agency, and has supported me with numerous other issues. But before her, I felt left out there to just fail! Now when I get overwhelmed and frustrated, she might not have the answer, but I have someone to call, vent to, and fight for me. Our foster son's CASA Worker is also amazing.

—Carey

To be sure, you will not need these all of these professionals and their services all the time, and for some children and placements, you may never need some of them. Nevertheless, there will be times that you do, as emergencies may arise when you do need a professional in any and all of these areas. Form a relationship with them now. Reach out to those you might not know. Pick up the phone and give them a call to introduce yourself; better yet, visit them in person. Let them know who you are and what you do, as a foster parent. Keep a list of their phone numbers and email addresses. We both know that, at any given moment and any given time, that the life of a foster parent is an unpredictable one. You never know when you might need help from someone in your professional support group.

Respite Care

There are those times when you might need or require a short-term break from the child for whom you are caring. This break, known as respite care, may be the result of a long-planned vacation that takes you out of the state, or even out of the country, that the child in foster care is unable to be a part of. Perhaps you are moving to a new home and need a temporary place for the child to stay while you are in transit between the old and new house. Maybe your own birth children require some much needed alone-time with you. Finally, you might just be trying to prevent burnout and need a break from their foster child. Other foster parents are often used for respite, as they are officially licensed to look after foster children and will be reimbursed for the interim that the foster child is placed in their home during the short break. Rest assured, respite is a welcome break for many foster parents and is an opportunity that you should not feel bad about taking advantage of. It is a normal part of the foster care process, and allows foster parents the opportunity to re-charge, as well as de-stress.

School Support

For quite some time, I was an English, History, and Drama high school teacher, both here in the United States and in Australia. When I first began teaching, and before I was a foster parent, I knew very little about foster care or about foster children. To be sure, what I thought I knew about children in foster care, and about the foster care system, was as far from the truth as possible. Like most of the general public, I had false ideas and beliefs about foster children, and much of it was negative, I am afraid to say. This was due mainly to the false stereotypes that abound in society. As a result, I was not prepared to meet the many needs that the students from foster homes so desperately needed while in my classroom. Even further, in all my years of college and additional instructional workshops, I did not have the training required to best help foster children as they struggled in my classroom, and neither did my colleagues. Most teachers are just like this, through no fault of their own.

After a few foster children had passed through my own home, I began to appreciate the fact that I had to not only adjust my teaching habits for foster children, but I also had to become my own foster children's advocate at their schools. I watched my foster children struggle in my fellow teacher's classrooms and was witness to these same teachers as they failed to understand the various emotional challenges that the children in my home were going through on a daily basis. To be sure, there were those times when I had to politely intervene on behalf of my foster child. There were also those times when I had to sit across the table from a fellow teacher as we discussed how my foster child's behavior was interfering in the classroom setting. My desire to better assist both my colleagues and foster children led to my doctoral studies on the subject. I simply wanted to help children in foster care succeed in school, as well as bring awareness about their struggles to our schools.

If you have heard me speak at foster care conferences or read some of my other books, then you know that one of my focuses is to help children in foster care with the many struggles they face in school. Foster children, in general, tend to perform below grade-level, in regards to both academic performance and positive behavior, than those students who come from traditional or economically disadvantaged homes. The majority of children under foster care supervision experience problems in behavior while enrolled in public schools. Those foster children who were taken from homes due to neglect repeatedly suffer from a number of developmental delays. These include poor language and vocabulary development, which serve to impair communication skills. My friend, this is only going to add to the challenges in your own home that you will face as a foster parent.

Here's the truth. Ready for it? For many children in foster care, our schools are the last place they want to be. Yet, most teachers and school administrators don't recognize or understand this. I have spoken to school system after school system across the nation on this subject. As it is in general society, and with our friends and family members, schools have those same false beliefs and assumptions about children in care.

For that foster child who has been taken from his family, from his home, from his friends, and all he knows, and is suddenly placed into a strange home late one evening, only to be forced to attend a strange school the following day, it is incredibly traumatic. Foster children often have a difficult time exhibiting proper school behavior during the school day. For many of the children, school is a constant reminder that they are, indeed, foster children without a true home. The continuous reminder that their peers are living with biological family members while they are not is a difficult reality for them, and can manifest itself in several ways. Some foster children simply withdraw and become anti-social in an attempt to escape their current environment and world they have been thrust into. For many foster children, violent behavior becomes the norm, as they not only act out in a negative and disruptive fashion in the school, but later on in your home, as well.

Since foster children are often behind academically and struggle with the fact that they are coming from outside school districts with different expectations, teachers in your child's school need to be conscious of this fact. Foster children struggle with many personal and emotional issues while in the foster home, and homework is often not the main objective while in the home each evening. Instead, the emotional issues your child faces may take center stage on a particular evening. Teachers need to assign homework with this in mind, being sensitive to their issues. Let your child's teacher know this, and ask that they cooperate with you. Meet with the teachers, the school counselor, and perhaps even an administrator of the school when you enroll your foster child and explain these concerns to them. Like I was beforehand, it is highly likely that they have not had much experience with foster children or the challenges they face.

As a foster parent, you will need to reach out to the teachers and ask for as much information and updates as possible. You need to create a support group of teachers, school counselors, and administrators, not only for the benefit of the child, but for your sake, as well. Reach out to the school and ask to meet with the teachers and other school employees that work with your child. Develop a relationship with them and give them some insight into the child's life and situation, so they can better understand him, his needs, and his challenges. Share your personal contact information with them and let them know they can call upon you in times of emergency with your child. Ask the same of them. It is essential to your child's success in school that you become actively involved and interested in your child's school life. As 55 percent of children in foster care drop out of school each year, according to a study by the Washington State Institute for Public Policy, it is most likely that your child will greatly struggle in school, thus causing you more difficulty and challenges as a foster parent. In order for the child in your home to not only thrive in school but also succeed, he will need your help, and you will need a support group from the school.

Free Stuff!

Not everyone can be a foster parent. You and I both know that. It is the hardest thing we do each day. However, everyone can help a child in foster care in some way. This I firmly believe. There are a number of ways for people to help children in need without actually taking them into their homes. Indeed, I have found that so many people, upon hearing the stories of the children, want to help a child in foster care, in some way. The exciting news is that more and more people and organizations are doing just that, which certainly helps both the child and you.

There is a thrift store in my town that has been helping foster parents and the kids in care for several years now. Each time a new child is placed into a home, foster parents know they can just pick up the phone and find help. There have been times when I have made those phone calls, as well. One time, my wife and I received a call requesting that we take a sibling group of three children into our home; a 6-month-old, a 2-year-old, and 4-year-old. After my wife and I agreed to help these three little ones out, and bring them into our family, I immediately picked up the phone and gave the thrift store a call. I was in need of two cribs and a small bed. I also needed some clothing and shoes to fit these children. I also needed another dresser for the younger two children. As the children were being dropped off at my house in 30 minutes time, you can imagine I was a little desperate for help. The thrift store was happy to donate all items for the children, and I raced off to pick them up. On the way there, I stopped by an insurance company, where the owner donated car seats to foster parents, and I picked up three brand new car seats.

Over and over again, I hear from foster parents who have had similar experiences. There are a number of foster care closets. Clothes closets offer for free gently-used or new clothing and apparel for children in foster care. Some clothes closets are set up like a business or clothing store, equipped with fitting rooms, and some even wrap or box the items, just like a true clothing store might. I have been in some foster care clothes closets throughout the country that offer items like jewelry, purses, and the latest fashions, while some also offer toiletries, and others might offer toys, school supplies, and other items a child might wish for or need.

Other organizations I have heard of host a school supply drive at the beginning of each year for the children placed into care in their community.

These organizations and non-profits donate paper, pencils, pens, note-books, rulers, calculators, and school bags to foster children. Still, another group donates suitcases to children in care in their area. There are also organizations that purchase gifts for children in foster care at Christmastime for the kids in their community. I have even spoken with organizations that offer free music and dance lessons to children from foster care. I just bet that you if ask around, or do some research on your own, you will find a group or a faith-based organization that helps children in foster care in some way in where you live.

Online Resources

We live in an age where we can find the answer to just about any question we might have through online technology. As a foster parent, this can be a wonderful tool and resource. Foster parents, in this digital age, can find support through a number of online platforms and social media. As I noted earlier in the chapter, there are countless foster parent support groups on social media for you to join, groups where you can find support. Along with this, there are online programs where you can gain training through online webinars. Indeed, I offer online training webinars, myself, through The Foster Care Institute. Additionally, you can go online and research on topics that interest you, as a foster parent, or want to learn more about. If the child in your home is suffering from a disorder or other complication, you can learn more about it online. As foster parents, you and I have the ability to learn and find support at the click of a button. My wife has found these most helpful, through the years, as she is unable to make many of our local training sessions through our agency and has instead gone online to get her hours, so to speak. Indeed, I continue to hear from foster parents across the nation who do the very same thing. Whether it is learning about grief and loss for foster parents, keeping children safe online, the dangers of human trafficking, or any number of other foster care related issues, online resources and training seminars can be very helpful for you, as a foster parent. To be sure, you can find online training webinars at The Foster Care Institute that cover these very issues and more.

CHAPTER 10

Inspiration as a Foster Parent

We have seen time and time again throughout this book that foster parenting is difficult. It's challenging. It's the hardest thing I have ever done, and maybe so for you, as well. From time to time, you and I need some words of hope, words of inspiration. This final chapter is just that, and one I hope you turn to when you need to find a reminder of why you have dedicated your life to helping children in need. To be sure, I have struggled myself at times, and these are words of inspiration that I have turned to, time and time again, and I have not only found strength from them, these words have also helped comfort me during difficult times, and have inspired me to continue during challenging times.

Thank you for what you do. Thank you for being a foster parent and caring for children. Thank you for opening your house, your home, your family, and your heart to children in need. Sadly, the need is strong, as there are so many children placed into care each year. Yet there are so few willing to be a foster parent, as it is not an easy task. Truly, it is the hardest job you will ever come to love.

Let's start with some great parenting quotes that I believe you will find both inspiring and relevant in your life as a foster parent. We begin with a powerful quote about what family truly means, by the late Princess Diana.

Parenting

"Family is the most important thing in the world."

— Princess Diana

"Affirming words from moms and dads are like light switches. Speak a word of affirmation at the right moment in a child's life and it's like lighting up a whole roomful of possibilities."

— Gary Smalley

"It's not only children who grow. Parents do too. As much as we watch to see what our children do with their lives, they are watching us to see what we do with ours. I can't tell my children to reach for the sun. All I can do is reach for it, myself."

— Joyce Maynard

"Life affords no greater responsibility, no greater privilege, than the raising of the next generation."

— C. Everet Koop, M.D.

"I don't think it matters how many parents you've got, as long as those who are around make their presence a good one."

— Elizabeth Wurtzel

"Fifty years from now it will not matter what kind of car you drove, what kind of house you lived in, how much you had in your bank account, or what your clothes looked like. But the world may be a little better place because you were important in the life of a child."

— Unknown

"Live so that when your children think of fairness and integrity, they think of you."

— H. Jackson Brown

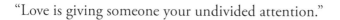

"Love is giving someone your undivided attention."

— Unknown

"Parenthood: it's not a job. It's an adventure!"

— Unknown

"The best inheritance a parent can give his children is a few minutes of his time each day."

— O. A. Battista

"The Hebrew word for parents is horim, and it comes from the same root as moreh, teacher. The parent is, and remains, the first and most important teacher that the child will have."

— Rabbi Kassel Abelson

Aren't those some amazing quotes? Now, we have some about children, and how they are truly a gift in each of our lives. Many of these quotes also point out how children need us, you and I, to love them with all that we have.

The Gift of Children

"Every child is gifted. They just unwrap their packages at different times."

— Unknown

"Kindness is the language which the deaf can hear and the blind can see."

— Mark Twain

"If a child is given love, he becomes loving ... If he's helped when he needs help, he becomes helpful. And if he has been truly valued at home ... he grows up secure enough to look beyond himself to the welfare of others."

— Dr. Joyce Brothers

"The greatest gift that you can give to others is the gift of unconditional love and acceptance."

— Brian Tracy

"When I approach a child, he inspires in me two sentiments; tenderness for what he is, and respect for what he may become."

— Louis Pasteur

"Children need love, especially when they do not deserve it."

— Harold Hulbert

"Children are likely to live up to what you believe in them."

— Ladybird Johnson

"All kids need is a little help, a little hope and somebody who believes in them."

— Earvin Magic Johnson

"A torn jacket is soon mended, but hard words bruise the heart of a child."

— Henry Wadsworth Longfellow

"Life, love, and laughter — what priceless gifts to give our children."

— Phyllis Dryden

"Every child comes with the message that God is not yet discouraged of man."

— Rabindranath Tagore

"While we try to teach our children all about life,
Our children teach us what life is all about."

— Angela Schwindt

" What is a home without children? Quiet."

— Henny Youngman

As we both know by now, foster parenting is challenging and it is difficult at times. I find the following quotes very important, as I often look to these to give me the strength I need during trials and times of difficulty.

In Difficult Times

"There are times when parenthood seems nothing but feeding the mouth that bites you."

— Peter de Vries

"There are two ways of meeting difficulties: you alter the difficulties or you alter the way you meet them."

— Phyllis Bottome

"Being disabled should not mean being disqualified from having access to every aspect of life."

— Emma Thompson

"Child abuse and neglect offend the basic values of our state. We have the responsibility to provide safe settings for at-risk children and facilitate permanent placement for children who cannot return home."

— Matt Blunt

"I went to law school. And I became a prosecutor. I took on the specialty that very few choose to pursue. I prosecuted child abuse and child homicide cases. Cases that were truly gut-wrenching. But standing up for those kids, being their voice for justice was the honor of a lifetime."

— Susana Martinez

"Childhood should be carefree, playing in the sun; not living a nightmare in the darkness of the soul."

— Dave Pelzer

"Survivors of abuse show us the strength of their personal spirit every time they smile."

— Jeanne McElvaney

"Cleaning your house while your kids are still growing up is like shoveling the walk before it stops snowing."

— Phyllis Diller

"Visualize the accomplishment of your everyday goals, and praise yourself each day for your hard work; never let a day pass without glorifying yourself for performing your duty as a parent."

— Kemmy Nola

"You don't always have to pretend to be strong.
There's no need to prove all the time that everything is going right.
You shouldn't be concerned about what other people are thinking.
Cry if you need to. It's good to cry out all your tears.
Because only then will you be able to smile again."

— Paul Coelho

My wife is amazing! She is, by far, the best mother and parent I have ever had the privilege to know. No matter how the child came to live with us and become a member of our family, my wife's motherly love has been an example to me. I am sure that you have had such mother figures in your life, as well. Indeed, you might just be that mother figure. Here are some great quotes about what it means to be a loving mother.

Foster Mothers

"The best part of being a mom to me is the unconditional love. I have never felt a love as pure, a love that is rewarding."

— Monica Denise Brown

"God could not be everywhere, therefore, he created mothers."

— Hebrew Proverb

"Biology is the least of what makes someone a mother."

— Oprah Winfrey

"Motherhood: All love begins and ends there."

— Robert Browning

"Mother love is the fuel that enables a normal human being to do the impossible."

— Marion C. Garretty

"Mothers hold their children's hands for a short while, but their hearts forever."

— Unknown

"The heart of a mother is a deep abyss at the bottom of which you will always find forgiveness."

— Honore de Balzac

"Of all the rights of women, the greatest is to be a mother.

— Lin Yutang, Chinese writer

"A mother is a person who seeing there are only four pieces of pie for five people, promptly announces she never did care for pie."

— Tenneva Jordan

"Few misfortunes can befall a boy which brings worse consequences than to have a really affectionate mother."

— W. Somerset Maugham

"Being a full-time mother is one of the highest salaried jobs ... since the payment is pure love."

— Mildred B. Vermont

"I remember my mother's prayers and they have always followed me. They have clung to me all my life."

— Abraham Lincoln

"Nobody knows of the work it makes
To keep the home together.
Nobody knows of the steps it takes,
Nobody knows- but Mother."

— Unknown

"And remember that behind every successful woman ... is a basket
of dirty laundry."

— Unknown

Okay, Dads, it's our turn. These are some special quotes for me, as they are
reminders of the importance of strong father figures in a child's life. I love
being a daddy, and I love having the opportunity to be a father figure to
children. I think our first quote, by Naveen Jain, sums it up about right.

Foster Fathers

"Being a father has been, without a doubt, my greatest source of
achievement, pride, and inspiration. Fatherhood has taught me
about unconditional love, reinforced the importance of giving
back, and taught me how to be a better person."

— Naveen Jain

"What Is A Dad?

A dad is someone who
wants to catch you before you fall
but instead picks you up,
brushes you off,
and lets you try again.

A dad is someone who
wants to keep you from making mistakes
but instead lets you find your own way,
even though his heart breaks in silence
when you get hurt.

A dad is someone who
holds you when you cry,
scolds you when you break the rules,
shines with pride when you succeed,
and has faith in you even when you fail ..."

— Unknown

"The righteous man walks in his integrity; his children are blessed after him."

— *Proverbs* 20:7

"Any man can be a Father but it takes someone special to be a dad."

— Anne Geddes

"My father didn't tell me how to live; he lived, and let me watch him do it."

— Clarence B. Kelland

"Every father should remember that one day his son will follow his example instead of his advice."

— Unknown

"It is not flesh and blood but the heart which makes us fathers and sons."

— Johann Schiller

"By profession I am a soldier and take pride in that fact. But I am prouder — infinitely prouder — to be a father. A soldier destroys in order to build; the father only builds, never destroys."

— Douglas MacArthur

Finally, we conclude this chapter with two poems about what foster parenting truly means. The first is from the perspective of a foster parent, while the second is from the perspective of a child that has been placed into foster care, and what that foster parent meant to the author.

Poems

Love Them Like They're Yours

Two brothers and a sister sit on the steps of their home
Being told they can no longer stay
Silent tears begin flowing
on each precious face as they slowly drive away
They drive to an office and sit in some chairs while a lady makes
calls on the phone
"They are really good kids," they hear her say "but right now they
need a substitute home."

Love them like they're yours
Even if just a little while
Love them like they're yours
Give them reasons to smile
They need you more than you can imagine
So Give them all you've got
... And love them like they're yours

A few hours later they pull up to a house with a nice yard a swing
and a van
They have no idea what they'll find inside, a friendly lady and man
Come in, you are welcome
To have a look around for now this is where you will stay
They can feel they are safe at this moment at least
And turn and go off to play

Love them like they're yours
Even if just for a while
Love them like they're yours
Give them reasons to smile
They need you more than you can imagine
So give them all you've got
... And love them like they're yours

Some time has gone by now and it's time to go Back
to the home they came from
Though it's a sad day your joy shines through
knowing in every way
You made them feel safe, independent, and strong
Gave them hope and love and peace
They turn and wave good-bye with a smile on their face knowing
it's okay to leave

Love them like they're yours
Even if just for a while
Love them like they're yours
Give them a reason to smile
They need you more than you can imagine
So give them all you've got
... And love them like they're yours

-

by

Marion Rhines

A Foster Parent's Poem

There I sat, alone and afraid,
You got a call and came right to my aid.
You bundled me up with blankets and love.
And, when I needed it most, you gave me a hug.
I learned that the world as not all that scary and cold.
That sometimes there is someone to have and to hold.
You taught me what love is, you helped me to mend.
You loved me and healed me and became my first friend.
And just when I thought you'd done all you do,
There came along not one new lesson, but two.
First you said, "Sweetheart, you're ready to go.

I've done all I can, and you've learned all I know."
Then you bundled me up with a blanket and a kiss.
Along came a new family, they even have kids!
They took me to their home, forever to stay.
At first I thought you sent me away.
Then that second lesson became perfectly clear.
No matter how far, you will always be near.
And so, Foster Mom, you know I've moved on.
I have a new home, with toys and a lawn.
But I'll never forget what I learned that first day.
You never really give your fosters away.
You gave me these thoughts to remember you by.
We may never meet again, and now I know why.
You'll remember I lived with you for a time.
I may not be yours, but you'll always be mine.

— Unknown

Glossary of Terms

The following terms come to us from the generosity of the WIN Family Services, who graciously gave permission to use these in this book.

Abuse - The physical, mental, or sexual injury of a child by a person, who may be any household or family member, who is responsible for the child's care or supervision, as well as any indications that a child's health or welfare is harmed or threatened.

Adoption - A legal process in which a person related or unrelated to a child becomes the adoptive family for that child and he/she is given all of the legal rights and privileges as if he/she were born to that family. The child's birth parents no longer have any legal responsibilities or rights after an adoption.

Adoptive Parents/Family - Persons who did not give birth to a child, but selected that child to be a member of their family. After a legal adoption, adoptive parents have all of the legal rights of natural parents.

Agency - A public or private organization providing a service.

Advocate - A person who acts or who speaks on behalf of another person to get things done for that person.

Anxiety - A feeling of being fearful, worried, or nervous. This may interfere with playing, learning, and a sense of well-being.

Assessment (also called evaluation) - The process of obtaining information from tests and observations.

Attorney (lawyer) - A person who will represent legal desires and interests while a child is in foster care.

Biological or Birth Parents - The parents who gave birth to a child who is placed in foster care.

Child Advocate - A person who gets to know the child and advocates for the best interest and the wishes of the child.

Child Protective Services (CPS) - A child welfare program responsible for investigating reports of child abuse and neglect as well as providing services to families in crisis. It is usually the first service that a child and family receive to prevent the child's removal from the home and placement in foster care.

Continuance - When there is an unresolved issue in the case, the court may continue services or delay a decision until the issue is resolve.

Counseling - Mental health services for individuals, families, couples, or other groups of people.

Court Liaison - The social worker attending uncontested court proceedings on behalf of the child's social worker.

Court Appointed Special Advocate (CASA) - A trained volunteer appointed by the court to ensure the safety of children in foster care and that they receive the services they need.

Custody - A legal term describing the legal right/responsibility of either a person or an agency to make decisions about where a child should live.

Depression - Sad or lonely feelings that are sometimes caused by a certain event or hormones in the body. It may interfere with a person's daily functions.

Eligibility - The determination that a child does or does not qualify to receive services based on certain rules.

Emancipation - The legal process by which a minor child petitions the court to allow him to become an adult in the eyes of the law before his 18th birthday.

Emergency Foster Care - Immediate placement in foster care because of a crisis related to a child or his/her family.

Family Conference - A group decision meeting to resolve issues such as visitation, placement of children, long term plans, emancipation, and re-unification plans.

Family Court - Deals with family matters such as custody, divorce, child support, etc.

Foster-Adoption - A foster family who requests to be considered to adopt a foster child.

Foster Child - A child up to age 18 in some states, and 21 years of age in other states placed in the care of a local department of social services by either a voluntary placement agreement with the birth family, adoptive family, legal guardian, or by a court commitment order.

Foster Care - A short-term service consisting of placing a child in a foster family home, group facility, or semi-independent living arrangement.

Foster Care Placement - An approved family home, a group home setting, or a residential treatment facility where a child will reside 24 hours a day and receive care, nurturing, and support.

Foster Parent - A relative or non-relative adult who is approved by the local department of social services to protect, nurture, educate, and care for a child.

Guardian Ad Litem (GLA) - A person the court appoints to investigate what solutions would be in the "best interests of a child."

GED (General Education Development) - A series of reading and math schoolwork, upon completion of which a diploma is conferred.

Home Study - An in-depth study of a potential adoptive family and their physical residence. Home studies are conducted by an Adoption Home Study Social Worker when a family has indicated that they want to be considered as an adoptive family.

Home Visit -Visits that are made by a caseworker in the home where the child lives or the home of the birth parents. Home visit refers to the location of the visit if it takes place in a home.

Individual Education Program (IEP) and Individualized Family Service Plan (IFSP) - Educational Services Plans that are developed by the school to provide needed special education services.

Jurisdictional Hearing - A hearing to determine if the child will be made a dependent of the Juvenile Court.

Juvenile Court - Deals with dependent children.

Mental Health Service - Services provided to assist individuals in identifying and resolving issues that impact one's thoughts and behaviors. The main goal is to make self-improvements and learn ways to cope with an individual's concerns.

Mentor - An individual who listens, supports, and encourages another individual. A mentor serves as a role model and helps a child get through difficult times.

Neglect - Not providing food clothing, shelter, health care, or education to a child.

Out-of-Home Placement - Short-term care that consists of 24-hour care and supervision as well as supportive services for a child whom the local department of social services has determined needs to live outside the home because the child has been abused, abandoned, neglected, or because his/her family is unable to provide care.

Parenting Class - Classes offered to parents to teach parenting skills and techniques. Often court ordered for birth parents.

Permanency Plan Hearing - A court hearing for all children in foster care that must occur within 11 months of coming into foster care and every six months after that until a child leaves foster care.

Reunification - When a foster child returns to his/her birth parents or relatives.

Residential Placement - A private or public group-type facility that provides 24-hour care for a child with medical or emotional needs.

Semi-independent Living Arrangement (SILA) - A placement in an apartment, room or college campus for a child to practice living independently.

Sibling Contact -Visitation between children in the same family. Often times sibling contact is ordered by the court or set up by the social worker(s).

Special Needs - Considered if a child has complex medical, behavioral, emotional needs, or developmental disabilities.

Substance Abuse Treatment - Generally counseling provided through a reputable treatment program to address drug and alcohol dependency and use/abuse. Often court ordered.

Supervised Visit - A visit between a child and a birth parent (or birth relative) that is conducted under the supervision of a third party.

Termination of Parental Rights (TPR) - When a judge signs an order that permanently ends the ties between a child and his/her parents.

Temporary Assistance to Needy Families (TANF) - Temporary funds to assist families that are in crisis and need financial help.

Treatment Foster Care (TFC) - A program in which foster parents are trained to provide care for children with disabilities or serious health care needs that require special services. Youth in treatment foster care have an extra caseworker (a TFC caseworker) that sees them once a week and helps them through crises.

Transition - The process of moving from one living arrangement to another.

Unsupervised Visit -Visitation between a child and his/her birth parent or relative without the supervision of a third party.

Voluntary Placement - When a child's parent or guardian places him/her temporarily in foster care by signing a voluntary placement agreement with the local department of social services instead of going to court. Voluntary placement provides care for a child when his/her parents are unable to do so. If a child is in foster care voluntarily for more than six months, the court will hold a hearing to decide whether or not he/she should remain in foster care.

Resources

Foster Care Contact Information:
CANADA

Canadian Foster Family Association

PO Box 2022
Yellowknife, NT X1A 2P5
Website: **http://www.canadian fosterfamilyassociation.ca**

Alberta Foster Parent Association

9488 51 Ave NW #303,
Edmonton, AB T6E 5A6,
Website: **http://www.afpaonline. com/**

British Columbia Federation of Foster Parent Associations

131 8th St
New Westminster, BC V3M 3P6,
Website: **http://www.bcfoster parents.ca/**

Manitoba Foster Family Network

90 Terracon Pl
Winnipeg, MB R2J 4G7
Website: **http://www.mffn.ca/**

New Brunswick Family and Community Services

551 King Street
Fredericton, NB E3B 1E7.
Website: **http://www2.gnb.ca/ content/gnb/en/departments/ social_development.html**

Newfoundland & Labrador Foster Families Association

21 Pippy Pl
St. John's, NL A1B 3X2
Website: **http://www.nlffa.com/**

Foster Family Coalition of the Northwest Territories

5125 50 St,
Yellowknife, NT X1A 1S2
Website: **http://www.ffcnwt.com/**

Foster Parents Society of Ontario

675 Hope Circle
Newmarket, Ontario L3X 1W3
Website: **http://www.
fosterparentssociety.org/**

Durham Foster Parent Association

3217 APPLING WAY
DURHAM, NC 27703.
Website: **https://www.guidestar.
org/profile/58-1563542**

Fédération des familles d'accueil du Québec

8500 Boulevard Henri-Bourassa
Bureau
256, Ville de Québec, QC G1G 5X1
Website: **http://ffariq.org/en**

Saskatchewan Foster Families Association

233 4th Ave S,
Saskatoon, SK S7K 1N1
Website: **http://www.sffa.sk.ca/**

Yellowknife Foster Family Association

5125 50 St,
Yellowknife, NT X1A 1S2
Website: **https://www.ffcnwt.
com/**

Foster Care Contact Information:
UNITED KINGDOM

London office

87 Blackfriars Road
London SE1 8HA
info@fostering.net

Cardiff office

1 Caspian Point
Pierhead Street
Cardiff Bay
CF10 4DQ
wales@fostering.net

Glasgow office

Ingram House
2nd floor
227 Ingram Street
Glasgow G1 1DA
scotland@fostering.net

Belfast office

Unit 10
40 Montgomery Road
Belfast BT6 9HL
ni@fostering.net

Foster Care Contact Information:
UNITED STATES OF AMERICA

Alabama Department of Human Resources

Center for Communications
Gordon Persons Building,
Suite 2104
50 North Ripley Street
Montgomery, AL 36130
Phone: 334 242-1310
Website: **http://dhr.alabama.gov/services/Foster_Care/FC_Children_Teens.aspx**

Alaska Health and Social Services

350 Main Street, Room 404
PO Box 110601
Juneau, Alaska 99811-0601
Phone: (907) 465-3030
Website: **http://hss.state.ak.us/ocs/fostercare/default.htm**

Arkansas Foster Family Services

P.O. Box 1437, Slot S560
Little Rock, AR, 72203-1437
Phone: 501-682-1442
Website: **http://www.fosterarkansas.org/**

Arizona Division of Children, Youth, and Families

P.O. Box 6123 Site Code 940A
Phoenix, AZ 85007
Phone: 877-543-7633
Website: **https://dcs.az.gov/**

California Department of Social Services

744 P Street
Sacramento, CA 95814
Phone: 916- 651-8788
Website: **http://www.cdss.ca.gov/**

Colorado Department of Human Services

1575 Sherman Street, 1st Floor
Denver, CO 80203-1714
Phone: 1-800-799-5876
Website: **https://www.colorado.gov/cdhs**

Connecticut Department of Children and Families

Commissioner's Office
505 Hudson Street
Hartford, CT 06106
Phone: 860-550-6300
Website: **http://www.portal.ct.gov/dcf**

Delaware Services for Children, Youth, and their Families

1825 Faulkland Road,
Wilmington, DE 19805
Phone: 302-451-2800
Website: **http://kids.delaware.gov/fs/fostercare.shtml**

District of Columbia Child and Family Services Agency

400 6th Street, SW
Washington, DC 20024
Phone: 202-442-6100
Website: **https://cfsa.dc.gov/**

Florida Department of Children and Families

100 Opa-locka Boulevard
Opa-locka, FL 33054
Phone: (305) 769-6324
Website: **http://www.myflfamilies.com/**

Georgia Department of Family and Children Services

2 Peachtree Street, NW
Suite 18-486
Atlanta, Georgia 30303
Phone: 404-651-9361
Website: **http://dfcs.dhs.georgia.gov/portal/site/DHS-DFCS/**

Hawaii Department of Human Services

Hui Ho'omalu
680 Iwilei Road, Suite 500
Honolulu, HI 96817
Phone: 1-888-879-8970
Website: **http://hawaii.gov/dhs/protection/social_services/child_welfare/Foster**

Idaho Department of Health and Welfare

PO Box 83720
Boise, ID 83720-0036
Phone: 800-926-2588
Website: **http://www.
healthandwelfare.idaho.gov/
Children/AdoptionFosterCare
Home/tabid/75/Default.aspx**

Illinois Department of Family and Children Services

406 East Monroe Street
Springfield, Illinois 62701
Phone: 1-800-572-2390
Website: **http://www.state.il.us/
dcfs/foster/index.shtml**

Indiana Department of Child Services

953 Monument Drive
Lebanon, IN 46052
Phone: 1-888-631-9510
Website: **http://www.in.gov/dcs/
index.htm**

Iowa Department of Human Services

1305 E. Walnut,
Des Moines, IA 50319-0114
Phone: 515-281-5521
Website: **http://www.dhs.iowa.gov/**

Kansas Department for Children and Families

230 E. William
Wichita, KS 67201
Phone: 785-296-4653
Website: **http://www.srs.ks.gov/
agency/Pages/
AgencyInformation.aspx**

Kentucky Cabinet for Health and Family Services

Office of the Secretary
275 E. Main St.
Frankfort, KY 40621
Phone: 1-800-372-2973
Website: **http://chfs.ky.gov/**

Louisiana Department of Children and Family Services

627 N. Fourth St.
Baton Rouge, LA 70802
Phone: 888-524-3578
Website: **http://www.dss.state.
la.us/**

Maine Office of Child and Family Services

2 Anthony Avenue
Augusta, Me 04333-0011
Phone: 207-624-7900
Website: **http://www.maine.gov/
dhhs/ocfs/**

Maryland Department of Human Services

311 West Saratoga St.
Baltimore, MD 21201
Phone: 410-767-7130
Website: **http://dhr.maryland. gov/**

Massachusetts Department of Children and Families

24 Farnsworth St.
Boston, MA 02210
Phone: 617-348-8400
Website: **http://www.mass.gov/ eohhs/gov/departments/dcf/**

Michigan Department of Human Services

Department of Human Services
235 S. Grand Ave. P.O. Box
30037 Lansing, Michigan 48909
Phone: 1-866-540-0008
Website: **http://www.mi.gov/ dhs/0,4562,7-124-60126---,00. html**

Minnesota Department of Human Services

PO Box 64244
St. Paul, MN 55164-0244
Phone: 651-431-3830
Website: **http://mn.gov/dhs/**

Missouri Department of Social Services

Broadway State Office Building
P.O. Box 1527
Jefferson City, MO 65102-1527
Telephone: 573- 751-4815
Website: **http://www.dss.mo.gov/ cd/fostercare/**

Mississippi Department of Human Services

750 N. State St.
Jackson, MS 39202
Phone: 601-359-4500
Website: **http://www.mdhs.state. ms.us/**

Nebraska Division of Children and Family Services

P.O. Box 95026
Lincoln, NE 68509-5044
Phone: (402) 471-9272
Website: **http://dhhs.ne.gov/ children_family_services/Pages/ children_family_services.aspx**

Nevada Division of Child and Family Services

4126 Technology Way, 3rd Floor
Carson City, NV 89706
Phone: 775-684-4400
Website: **http://dcfs.state.nv.us/**

New Hampshire Department of Health and Human Services

129 Pleasant St.
Concord, NH 03301-3852
Phone: 800-894-5533
Website: **http://www.dhhs.nh. gov/dcyf/index.htm**

New Jersey Department of Children and Families

20 West State Street, 4th floor
PO Box 729
Trenton, NJ 08625-0729
Phone: 877-652-0729
Website: **http://www.state.nj.us/ dcf/index.shtml**

New Mexico Children, Youth, and Families Department

P.O. Drawer 5160
Santé Fe, MN 87502-5160
Phone: 800-432-2075
Website: **https://cyfd.org/**

New York Office of Children and Family Services

52 Washington St.
Renssleaer, NY 12144-2736
Phone: 518-473-7793
Website: **http://ocfs.ny.gov/main/**

North Carolina Department of Health and Human Services

2001 Mail Service Center
Raleigh, NC 27699-2001
Phone: 919-855-4800
Website: **http://www.ncdhhs.gov/ childrenandyouth/index.htm**

North Dakota Department of Children and Family Services

600 East Boulevard Avenue
Department 325
Bismarck ND 58505-0250
Phone: 701-328-2316
Website: **http://www.nd.gov/dhs/ services/childfamily/**

Ohio Department of Jobs and Family Services

30 E. Broad Street, 32nd Floor
Columbus, Ohio 43215
Phone: 614-466-1213
Website: **http://jfs.ohio.gov/ ocomm_root/0002OurServices. stm**

Oklahoma Division of Children and Family Services

Sequoyah Memorial Office Building
2400 N. Lincoln Blvd.
Oklahoma City, OK 73105
Phone: 405-552-1487
Website: **http://www.okdhs.org/ services/cws/Pages/default.aspx**

Oregon Department of Human Services

500 Summer St. NE E62
Salem, OR 97301-1067
Phone: 503-945-5944
Website: **http://www.oregon.gov/ DHS/children/**

Pennsylvania Department of Public Welfare

625 Forster Street
Harrisburg, PA 17120
Phone: 800-692-7462
Website: **http://dhs.pa.gov/**

Rhode Island Department of Human Services

Louis Pasteur Building #57
600 New London Avenue
Cranston, RI 02920
Phone: 401-462-2121
Website: **http://www.dhs.ri.gov/**

South Carolina Department for Children and Families

P.O. Box 1520
Columbia, SC 29202-1520
Phone: 803-898-7601
Website: **https://dss.sc.gov/ content/customers/index.aspx**

South Dakota Department of Social Services

700 Governors Drive
Pierre, SD 57501
Phone: 605-773-3165
Website: **https://dss.sd.gov/**

Tennessee Department of Children's Services

Cordell Hull Building, 7th Floor
Nashville, TN 37243
Phone: 615-741-9701
Website: **https://www.tn.gov/dcs. html**

Texas Department of Family and Protective Services

701 W. 51st St
Austin, TX 78751
Phone: 1-800-233-3405
Website: **http://www.dfps.state. tx.us/**

Utah Department of Child and Family Services

195 North 1950 West
Salt Lake City, Utah 84116
Phone: 801-538-4100
Website: **https://dcfs.utah.gov/**

Vermont Department for Children and Families

103 South Main Street,
2 & 3 North
Waterbury, VT 05671-5500
Phone: 800-649-2642
Website: **http://dcf.vermont.gov/**

Virginia Department of Social Services

801 E. Main Street
Richmond, VA 23219-2901
Phone: 800-468-8894
Website: **http://www.dss.virginia. gov/family/fc/index.cgi**

Washington Department of Social and Health Services

PO Box 45130
Olympia, WA 98504-5130
Phone: 800-737-0617
Website: **http://www.dshs.wa. gov/ca/general/index.asp**

West Virginia Children and Family Services

350 Capitol Street, Room 691
Charleston, West Virginia 253013704
Phone: 304-558-3431
Website: **http://dhhr.wv.gov/bcf/ Pages/default.aspx**

Wisconsin Department of Children and Families

201 East Washington Avenue,
Second Floor
P.O. Box 8916
Madison, WI 53708-8916
Phone: 608-267-3905
Website: **http://dcf.wisconsin.gov/**

Wyoming Department of Family Services

2451 Foothill Blvd., Suite 103
Rock Springs, WY 82901
Phone: 307-352-2509
Website: **http://dfsweb.state. wy.us/protective-services/foster- care/index.html**

National Foster Parent Association

1102 Prairie Ridge Trail
Pflugerville, Texas 78660
Phone: 800-557-5238
Website: **www.nfpaonline.org**

Publications:

Foster Focus Magazine

Foster Focus Magazine
608 Main Street
Watsontown, PA 17777
570-538-3608
Email: **info@FosterFocusMag.com**
Website: **http://fosterfocusmag.com/aboutus.html**

Represent: The Voice of Youth in Foster Care

Represent Magazine
242 W. 38th St., 6th floor
New York, NY 10018
212-279-0708 x112

Fostering Families Today

412 W. 6th St. Suite 925,
Los Angeles, CA 90014.
888-924-6736.
Website: **www.fosteringfamiliestoday.com**

Organizations

Becca's Closet

151 North Nob Hill Road
Suite 280
Plantation, FL 33324
(954) 424-9999

Foster Care Closet

643 S25th Street,
Suite 8 Lincoln Nebraska 68510
Website: fostercarecloset.org

Foster Closet

8307 Beach Blvd
Jacksonville, FL 32216
Website: www.fostercloset.org

Hope in a Suitcase

311 N. Robertson Blvd. PO Box #715
Beverly Hills, CA 90211
Website: http://www.hopeinasuitcase.org/

Hands of Hope Adoption and Orphan Care Ministry

4350 Mundy Drive,
Suite 800 #119,
Noblesville, IN 46060
855.464.4673

Kids in the New Groove

Address: 2906 S 1st St #306,
Austin, TX 78704
Phone: (512) 596-5441

OneHope27

Website: **https://www.
onehope27.org/**

Orphan Solutions

28918 S. Plum Creek Dr.
Spring, Texas 77386
Phone (281) 465-8122
Website: **https://www.
orphancaresolutions.com/**

Royal Family Kids

3000 W. MacArthur Blvd,
Suite 412
Santa Ana, CA 92704
Website: **www.rfk.org**

South Carolina Youth Advocate Program

140 Stoneridge Dr. Ste 350
P: 803-744-6494
F: 803-779-8444
Website: **www.scyap.com**

Uplift Family Services

251 Llewellyn Ave.Biop
Campbell CA 95008
Website: **https://upliftfs.org/**

Win Family Services

2502 W. Northern Parkway
Baltimore, MD 21215
Website: http://winfamilyservices.
org/

Works Cited

Dale, G., Kendall, J.C., Humber, K., & Sheehan, L. (1999). Screening young foster child for posttraumatic stress disorder and responding to their needs for treatment. APSAC Advisor, 12(2).

DeGarmo, J. (2013) The Foster Parenting Manual: A Practical Guide to Creating a Loving, Safe, and Stable Home. Jessica Kingsley Publishers.

Spears, W. and Cross, M., 2003. How do 'children who foster' perceive fostering? Adoption and Fostering, 27(4), pp.38-45.

Twigg, R. and Swan, T., 2007. What research tells us about the experience of foster carers' children. Adoption and Fostering, 31(4), pp.49-61.

Watson, A, Jones, D, 'The impact of fostering on foster carers' own children', Adoption & Fostering 26:1, pp 49–55, 2002.

Educational Outcomes of Foster Youth-Benchmarks. Washington State Institute for Public Policy.

WIN Family Services. (2014) Foster Care Terms. Retrieved from http://www.winfamilyservices.org/terms-and-fostercare

About the Author

Dr. John DeGarmo has been a foster parent for 15 years, and he and his wife have had over 50 children come through their home. He is an international consultant to legal firms and foster care agencies, as well as an empowerment and transformational speaker and trainer on many topics about the foster care system. He is the author of several foster care books, including *Love and Mayhem: One Big Family's Uplifting Story of Fostering and Adoption*, and writes for several publications. Dr. DeGarmo and his wife have been honored with the Good Morning America Ultimate Hero Award, the Up With People Everyday Hero Award, and other honors.

He can be contacted at **drjohndegarmo@gmail**, through his Facebook page, Dr. John DeGarmo, or at The Foster Care Institute.

Made in United States
Orlando, FL
19 April 2024

45966154R00100